The Vale of Pewsey

The Vale of Pewsey

John Chandler

First published in the United Kingdom in 1991; 2nd edition 2000
This revised and expanded 3rd edition published in 2018

by The Hobnob Press,
8 Lock Warehouse, Severn Road, Gloucester GL1 2GA
www.hobnobpress.co.uk

British Library Cataloguing in Publication Data
A catalogue record for this book is available from the British Library

ISBN 978-1-906978-56-3

Typeset in Chaparral Pro.
Typesetting and origination by John Chandler

Printed by Lightning Source

Front cover picture:
'Adam's Grave' print by Jenny Ford, reproduced by kind permission of the artist

Title page:
Spring in the Vera Jeans Nature Reserve, Jones's Mill, Pewsey, with Martinsell beyond (author)

CONTENTS

For Ruth

About the Author

JOHN CHANDLER was born in 1951 and brought up in Devon. He studied classics at the University of Bristol, and was awarded his doctorate for research there on ancient history in 1977. Between 1974 and 1988 he worked for Wiltshire County Council, from 1979 as Local Studies Librarian, based at Trowbridge. Since 1988 he has worked as a freelance historical researcher, writer and lecturer, latterly (since 2011) for the Victoria County History in Gloucestershire and Wiltshire. He has written or edited more than twenty books, including histories of Salisbury, Swindon and churches in Wiltshire, and editions of the travellers John Leland and John Taylor. He is a Fellow of the Society of Antiquaries and is a publisher of books on local and regional history: www.hobnobpress. co.uk. He lives in Gloucester.

The Cover Artist

JENNY FORD studied at The Ealing School of Art, and Fine Art (painting) at the Central School of Art and Design, where she developed a passion for printmaking. In 1973 she moved to Wiltshire, where she was captivated by the landscape and the local prehistoric sites, which heavily influenced her work. In 2017 she relocated to Flintshire in North Wales, to a studio with views of hills and across to the sea. For further information about Jenny and her work visit her website: www. jennyfordprintmaker.co.uk.

INTRODUCTION TO
THE THIRD EDITION

THIS WAS ALWAYS a favourite among my books – not through any qualities inherent in its writing, but because of the subject. The scenery it describes, the Vale of Pewsey, invites the explorer to begin with its geological origins, then admire the bounty harvested from its soil, and move on to observe the boundaries imposed and settlements set down by those who have exploited and loved it, rich and poor. From faceless names and statistics the people of the Vale emerge on to this stage first as individuals going about their business, indulging their pleasures, and making sense (or nonsense) of their surroundings; and then as personalities – characters we can all relate to. My book simply follows this great progress, and records what I have discovered on the way.

The book was conceived nearly thirty years ago, when Roger Jones, publisher of Ex Libris Press, wished to begin a series of titles describing 'West Country Landscapes' and approached me to contribute. For my own projected series of Wiltshire books I had recently been exploring and researching parishes around Devizes and Marlborough, and so had material at hand. But the deeper reason for choosing to write about the Vale of Pewsey was that I felt, and still feel, that this is the true heart of Wiltshire, geographically, but also – as I suggested in my original introduction – emotionally, if by that one means that it embodies the essence of the rural county. It is a land of great beauty and subtle charms, still largely unexplored by the tourist – unless by canal boat – but prized and cherished by all who live in it or near it. It was also, I felt then, rather neglected by historians and country writers, and I could cite only one book, published in 1954, devoted specifically to the Vale.

North and south the Vale of Pewsey is clearly defined by the chalk escarpments of the Marlborough Downs and Salisbury Plain respectively.

East and west the limits are less clear, and I have drawn my line at Burbage in the east, where Savernake Forest begins, and the fringes of Devizes in the west. But I have also tracked south a little to include the Lavingtons and Potterne. The presence of Devizes, as the market town to which most of the Vale resorts, is acknowledged from time to time, but does not intrude. Devizes has its own books aplenty.

The Vale of Pewsey was published in 1991 and sold steadily in the modest way that local histories do, until a second edition was required in 2000. I made small changes to it then and its appearance was improved by Ex Libris, who reissued it. Out of print for some years, it seems a good time to publish a third edition (under my own imprint, Hobnob Press), which can benefit from advances in printing technology to show the Vale off in colour, and must also try to bring the story up to date. Not only has life here moved on (though less so than in many other places), but much more has been studied, discovered and written about the Vale, and ideas about landscape history prevalent when I first expounded them have been challenged and modified. I tip my hat to these modifications, and have sometimes altered my text accordingly. But as a general rule I remain wedded to the dictum of W.G. Hoskins, that 'everything in the landscape is older than we think', even though some things, it now seems, are perhaps not.

I too am older than most people think (myself included sometimes), though probably no wiser, and I am profoundly thankful that I have been able to explore the Vale again on foot, three decades later, to visit and re-photograph the same places, and to revise and supplement the walks. I have added two walks to the previous four, and when you have read my book I would urge you – if you are able – to go out and explore the lanes and footpaths of the Vale for yourself. It has lost none of its quiet magic, and in early summer (when I took all the photographs) there is nowhere I would sooner be.

Most of the helpers I acknowledged in the previous editions have moved on, in one way or another, but my gratitude remains: in alphabetical order Betty Andrews, Alison Borthwick, Hilda and Alec Choules, Clare Conybeare, Felicity Gilmour, Katharine Jordan, Derek Parker, Frances Price; not to mention the victims of my various adult education classes at Pewsey, Marlborough and Urchfont, and (inevitably) my dog Lily. Roger Jones, my erstwhile publisher, has encouraged me to produce this new edition, as has my wife Ruth Smalley, and to both I am grateful for their support. In addition to thanking the staff of the Wiltshire and Swindon History Centre and the Wiltshire Museum for their continued friendship and wisdom, I must also now acknowledge my colleagues in the Victoria County History, past and present, in Wiltshire, Gloucestershire and London, for enriching my understanding of local history.

John Chandler
Gloucester
August 2018

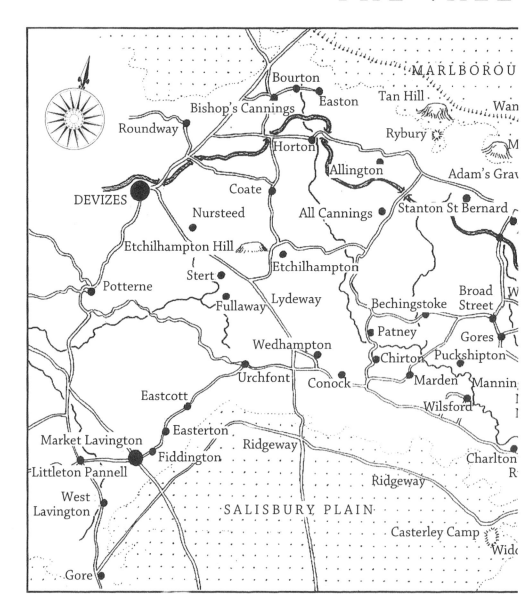

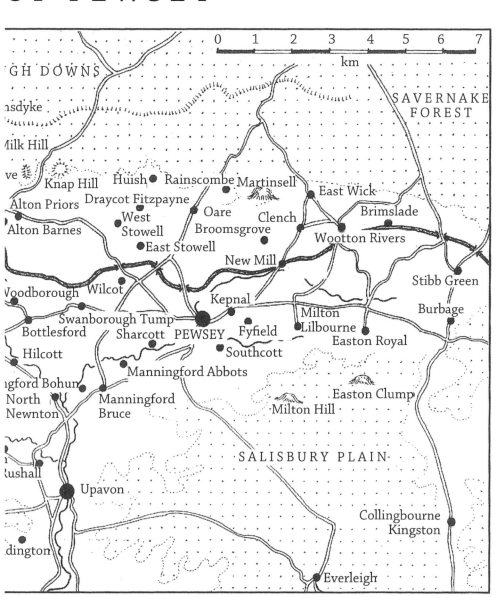

GH DOWNS

SAVERNAKE
FOREST

sdyke

Milk Hill

ve
Knap Hill Huish Rainscombe Martinsell
Alton Priors Draycot Fitzpayne
West Oare Clench
Alton Barnes Stowell Broomsgrove
East Stowell
New Mill
Woodborough Wilcot
Kepnal
Swanborough Tump
Bottlesford Sharcott PEWSEY Fyfield
Hilcott Southcott
Manningford Abbots
gford Bohun
North Manningford
Newton Bruce Milton Hill

East Wick
Brimslade
Wootton Rivers
Stibb Green
Burbage
Milton
Lilbourne
Easton Royal
Easton Clump

SALISBURY PLAIN

ushall
Upavon
dington

Collingbourne
Kingston

Everleigh

0 1 2 3 4 5 6 7
km

'Old Adam' – Adam's Grave, a Neolithic long barrow on Walker's Hill

1
A WIDE COUNTRY

'I AM JUST RETURNED from the top of Old Adam,' wrote Maria Hare to a friend in December 1831, 'having thought of you as I can scarce help doing always on those green sloping Downs, with all that wide country spread below one; and watching, not the busy gleaners and the waggons loading, but the slow, toilsome plodding of the horses and oxen at the plough.' Maria's story will be told later, but her vantage point, the neolithic long barrow which she called Old Adam, and which we know as Adam's Grave, is the most appropriate place to begin this account of the Vale of Pewsey. It stands on Walker's Hill, a chalk spur above the twin villages of Alton Barnes and Alton Priors, not far from a road, and freely accessible to all within the Pewsey Downs nature reserve (see Walk 4). The view from its gentle turf encompasses nearly everywhere described in this book, and the feeling of exhilaration today is no less than Maria Hare felt in 1831. 'The soft mild air and autumn gleams make one's position so high above all earthly fogs and smoke as wholesome for mind as body, and I am come home all the better for the pure air I breathed there.'

The Vale of Pewsey separates Wiltshire's two principal areas of chalk downland, Salisbury Plain to the south and the Marlborough Downs to the north. It extends for rather more than 20km across the centre of Wiltshire from the neighbourhood of Devizes in the west to the edge of Savernake Forest in the east. Its width varies between about 6km and 10km, narrowing as you travel east along it. The floor of the Vale is lower along its southern edge, around 100m above sea level, and the southern chalk escarpment is also lower than its northern counterpart, rarely exceeding a height of 200m. As you cross the Vale to the north the ground rises slowly so that the steep, indented hills which form its northern edge rise from around 150m to nearly 300m in places. Devizes

View from Milk Hill along the escarpment eastward, including Walker's Hill, Knap Hill, Huish Hill, Giant's Grave and Martinsell.

at the western end and Wootton Rivers near the eastern end both lie at about 130m above sea level, which enabled the stretch of the Kennet and Avon Canal linking them to be channelled along the Vale without a single change of level. Stert, a small exquisite village near the Vale's western entrance, by my reckoning lies at the true geographical centre of the county of Wiltshire.

Walker's Hill, Old Adam's resting place, is one of several chalk promontories which jut from the Vale's northern skyline. Standing on the barrow one's view westward along the ragged escarpment takes in Milk Hill (with its white horse engraved in the chalk) and Tan Hill, Rybury which projects into the Vale, and beyond it in the distance Roundway Hill overlooking Devizes. Milk Hill and Tan Hill both exceed 290m. They share the honour of being the highest points in Wiltshire, and fall only three metres short of Walbury in Berkshire, the highest place in central southern England. Roundway stands sentinel at the western end of the Vale; its counterpart, as the eye looks eastward beyond neighbouring Knap Hill, is the commanding dome of Martinsell, which sees and is seen by all the Vale east of Pewsey, and can even be discerned more than 25km distant across Salisbury Plain when driving on the A303 near Winterbourne Stoke. From Adam's Grave Roundway is 11km away, and Martinsell is 6km.

Looking across the Vale now, its southern edge has the appearance of a wall. This is the scarp of Salisbury Plain, and from here it seems to be continuous from Easton Clump in the east to Urchfont Hill in the west, some 18km. On closer inspection, however, it is less regular than the distant view suggests. The hills are wrinkled and gouged like some giant mural sculpture; the scarp is not in fact continuous, but is punctuated half-way along at Upavon by the beginnings of a river valley; and it does not end at Urchfont Hill, but merely turns more southerly, and continues in the same way out of the Vale to Westbury and beyond.

There are other, less significant chalk hills rising from the floor of the Vale itself. The unmistakable profiles of tree-topped Woodborough Hill and the almost conical Picked (or Pecked) Hill lie south of Adam's Grave, and looking away to the west the view between Roundway and

Picked (Pecked) Hill from the south, by Ladies Bridge near Wilcot

Urchfont is closed by Etchilhampton Hill. Far away, to east and west, more distant horizons may be seen on clear days – the Cotswolds, the Mendips, the Hampshire Downs. Alfred's Tower, on the border of Wiltshire and Somerset, is just discernible, and they say (although I am incredulous) that with a telescope so is the spire of Salisbury Cathedral.

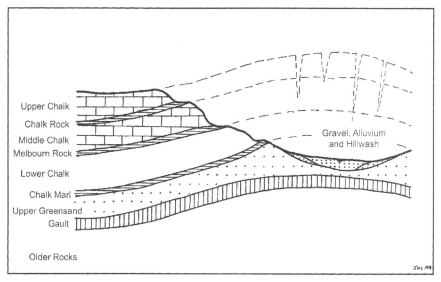

A simplified geological cross-section across the Vale (not to scale)

This then is the skyline that Old Adam offers. But how has it come to be like this? The geology of Pewsey Vale, the rocks which form the stage for all its subsequent dramas of life, can be understood at a fairly basic level without too much difficulty. Chalk, Upper Greensand and Gault Clay are the three rocks principally involved. All three are known as cretaceous, and were deposited by the sea between about 150 and 65 million years ago. The gradually changing extent of this sea dictated the types of minerals fed into it by rivers and the nature of the marine life which lived and died there. Hence the Gault (the oldest of the three) has different properties from the Greensand overlying it, and the Chalk (the youngest) is very different again. And there are further distinctions: the Chalk is divided into three bands – Lower (or Grey Chalk), and Middle and Upper (White Chalk) – and between them are thin layers of harder substances, known as Melbourn Rock (between Lower and Middle Chalk) and Chalk Rock (between Middle and Upper Chalk). Another intermediate layer, known as Chalk Marl, separates the Upper Greensand from its overburden of Chalk. Naturally other, older rocks underlie those which outcrop in the Vale of Pewsey, and in places superficial deposits of more recent material mantle the solid geology, as we shall see.

Long after this sequence of rocks had been deposited, and the sea had retreated (very roughly 25 million years ago), pressure from below caused the land to buckle, and produced in southern England a series of corrugations running from east to west. The Vale of Pewsey was caused by one such upward fold, known as an anticline. Along its axis (the bulge or ridge of the corrugation) the upper strata of rocks were stretched to the point of fracture, and the resulting cracks rendered them vulnerable to weathering and erosion, especially by frost. In course of time the Chalk disintegrated and exposed the Greensand, and as the valley took shape along this line of weakness a river began to flow in it, gentle stream or raging torrent by turns, and thus accelerated the erosion process and further modified the landscape. But before considering in more detail the rivers of the Vale it is time to return to our vantage point on Adam's Grave.

View near Allington on the Lower Chalk to the northern escarpment and Tan Hill

Much of the floor of the Vale, the wide country stretching away before us, consists of Upper Greensand, which has been exposed by the removal through weathering of the overlying sequence of Chalk strata. But there are a number of exceptions and modifications to this general rule. Towards the western end of the Vale, beyond Urchfont, the Greensand too has been eroded, and here the Gault and earlier rocks are exposed. Conversely at the extreme eastern end of the Vale, where the trees of Savernake Forest show black in the far distance, erosion never entirely conquered the Chalk, so that the Greensand remains buried. Elsewhere, too, remnants of the overlying Chalk have survived as outliers, and take the form of stranded peaks rising from the Vale itself. Etchilhampton Hill, Woodborough Hill and Picked Hill fall into this category, as well as the modest swelling east of Beechingstoke which is known as Stoke Elm.

On either side of the valley floor, where the ground begins to slope upwards to meet the downs, there is a band of Lower Chalk, varying in width from a half to three or more kilometres. To the south

Etchilhampton Hill from the south, a Lower Chalk outlier surrounded by Greensand

Rainscombe House, north of Oare, encircled by the steep Chalk escarpment

the impressive scarp wall seen across the Vale from Adam's Grave is composed of Lower Chalk, here capped by the thin layer of harder Melbourn Rock, which provides its characteristically level top. The loftier northern scarp continues above this harder layer to bring to the surface bands of Middle and Upper Chalk. It has more and greater indentations than its counterpart, in the form of coombes and dry valleys; Rainscombe House, north of Oare, for instance, stands like a prima donna dwarfed by a vast encircling auditorium of chalk.

Mention of valleys brings us back to the question of rivers, because water is the other factor in this geological equation. The layers of Chalk and Greensand are porous, and so soak up and store rainfall, but the Gault Clay is not, and nor is the Chalk Marl between the Lower Chalk and the Greensand. Springs therefore issue in two bands, above and below the junction between Chalk and Greensand; they flow as streams to join the principal rivers of the Vale, the two headwaters of the Salisbury or Christchurch Avon. In general rain falling on the Marlborough Downs between the Kennet valley and Pewsey Vale gravitates to the Vale, because it is lower than the Kennet, whereas

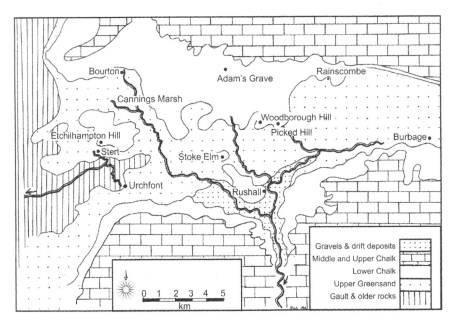

The geology and drainage of the Vale

rain falling on Salisbury Plain finds its way to the winterbournes and
rivers further south. Consequently most water flowing in Pewsey Vale is
derived from the hills to the north, and so the northern escarpment has
more valleys and indentations than the southern.

The two Rivers Avon, one flowing east from Fishwater at Bourton
above Bishop's Cannings, the other flowing west from Seymour Pond
and various sources near Burbage, join forces near Scales Bridge, Rushall,
and their mingled waters decide to turn south, leaving the Vale by an
opening which they have cleft in the Chalk downland of Salisbury Plain.
Before this exit became available, however (probably as a result of sea-
level changes some two million years ago), it is believed that the upper
Avon was a single river flowing east to the sea via the Bedwyn area east
of Burbage. The principal source of this river was probably a marshy area
at the north-western end of the Vale. This was Cannings Marsh, as it was
known when the Anglo-Saxon Chronicle recorded a Danish raid there in
the 11th century, and it probably centred on the often-waterlogged flat
valley floor between Coate, Etchilhampton and All Cannings. The names
of two nearby villages, Horton and Patney, derive from words implying
waterlogged terrain.

But there is another river system which also helps to drain the Vale. It rises at Urchfont and Stert, and flows westwards near Potterne to swell the Bristol – rather than the Salisbury – Avon. It descends more rapidly than the languid streams further east, and one effect of this has been that over time it is cutting back its valley to encroach eastwards along the Vale. A sudden change of direction in the flow of a stream from east to west between Stert and Fullaway (see Walk 2) can be explained as the capture of an east-flowing tributary of the Salisbury Avon by the more vigorous west-flowing tributary of the Bristol Avon. In its valley this tributary has succeeded in cutting down through the Gault Clay which outcrops in the Urchfont area to expose the older rocks beneath, Portland Sands and Kimmeridge Clay.

Water has had other effects on the landscape of the Vale. Although not covered by permanent ice during periods of glaciation, Wiltshire experienced (most recently about 10,000 years ago) the scouring and eroding effects of rapidly melting snow. This not only helped to sculpt the escarpments; it also deposited soil and rock from the hillsides on

The escarpment on Milk Hill sculpted by glacial meltwaters

to the floor of the Vale. And so we find areas of chalky and clayey drift deposits caused by melt water and hillwash at various places. In addition the streams and rivers in spate have carried down and deposited on their floodplains gravels and alluvium which, like the other drift deposits, serve to mask the underlying geological structure and affect the uses to which the land may be put by plants, animals and man.

Our view from 'Old Adam' has been long in the making, and across the vastnesses of geological time natural forces continue their work of modification and change. But if all we see are the profiles of the hills defining the wide country of the Vale, then our vision will be blinkered indeed. We have not yet noticed the fields and trees, the houses, lanes and villages. But we have grappled with the basic structure of the landscape, and now that we can understand some of its causes we are ready to begin exploring their effects.

2

LAND OF PROMISE

THIS CHAPTER, IN which we examine the agriculture and ecology of the Vale, may best begin like the last, with an individual describing a view. In 1826, five years before Maria Hare's visit to Old Adam, William Cobbett rose early on an August morning to ride north from Everleigh, across the downs to the escarpment above Milton Lilbourne. From here (see Walk 3), overlooking Milton, Easton and Pewsey, the old political crusader saw what he described as, 'my land of promise; or, at least, of great expectation'. Spread out before him was an agricultural regime which, much modified, had existed for many centuries.

> The shape of the thing is this: on each side downs, very lofty and steep in some places, and sloping miles back in other places. From the edge of the downs begin capital arable fields generally of very great dimensions, and, in some places, running a mile or two back into little cross valleys, formed by hills of downs. After the corn-fields come meadows, on each side, down to the brook, or river. The farm-houses, mansions, villages, and hamlets, are generally situated in that part of the arable land which comes nearest the meadows.

Cobbett's recognition of the three basic types of agricultural land, the downland for rough grazing, the hillsides for arable, and the meadows for rich pasture, is basic to the Vale's history, and is of course related to its geology. But not directly related – the most important factor is the soil, and that depends on climate, previous plant and animal life and human activity, as well as on the solid and drift geology underneath. In the Vale the drift deposits are particularly important. They occur as chalky gravels carried down the hillsides some

I WILL LIFT UP MINE
EYES UNTO THE HILLS
FROM WHENCE
COMETH
MY HELP

IN MEMORY OF
MARGARET AND
ISABELLA
NIVEN
CHARLES THEIR

NEPHEW AND
MABEL HIS WIFE
ALL OF
MARDEN GRANGE
1900 1952

ten millennia ago as the last ice age receded, and often overlain by a loamy brown clay known as brickearth. Patches of this gravel deposit are widespread, especially from Marden eastwards to Rushall, and then beside the road up to Pewsey. Further west, in the Lydeway area, a greyish clay drift overlies the Gault; and along the banks of streams and rivers there are strips of alluvial silt.

Wind and water have broken up, transported and mixed the solid rocks and drift deposits at the surface, to provide a medium in which plants could root and become established; and their detritus in turn contributed to the fertility of this developing soil. Over time a great variety of soils evolved (a survey of part of the Vale has identified 29 different soil series); these could support an abundant flora and fauna, and in due course enabled people to use the land for agriculture. The history of soil and early land use can be studied archaeologically, and this was done when Marden Henge was investigated in 1969.

above: Part of the bank of Marden Henge can be seen from the road bridge across the Avon, north of the village, although it is shrouded in trees

left: The Vale of Pewsey landscape depicted in modern glass in Marden church

Since that excavation was carried out the major significance of the henge itself, and of Hatfield barrow, the 'superbarrow' which once stood inside it, has been recognised. In consequence a great deal of research has been undertaken to find evidence of, and to understand, the prehistoric society and economy that surrounded it in the Vale. Little tangible evidence of settlement in the Vale itself has been found from the Neolithic and Bronze Age periods, although there was clearly a significant population that created and assembled at ritual monuments and commemorated their dead. Our concern in this chapter is not with the archaeological discoveries as such, but with what they tell us about the evolution of the farming landscape.

At Marden, on the valley floor, archaeologists determined that the solid geology, Upper Greensand, was covered during the last ice age by four distinct deposits of chalky drift material, probably washed down from the northern escarpment. The earliest layer contained the remains of snails whose presence suggests a cold, open, treeless landscape with some marshy ground and temporary pools. The second and third layers were barren, but the latest deposit also contained snails which lived in a cold, marshy environment. This sequence suggests a cold climate which became unbearably so during the last ice age, and then warmed to permit life to return. As the ice retreated and the temperature improved the Vale became clothed in forest, and a soil evolved over some 6,000-10,000 years which supported and was in part created by the trees. Then around 5,000 years ago human activity, in clearing areas of forest for cultivation, led to a different soil, a sandy loam which in time became impermeable, and would have caused waterlogged conditions unsuitable for agriculture. The barren period continued at Marden for some seven centuries, until the soil sequence was buried by the henge builders in about 2,000 BC.

This sketch of the prehistoric valley landscape can be set beside a hillside perspective derived from an excavation in 1961 at Knap Hill. This is the causewayed enclosure which overlooks Alton, and it was probably built during the forest clearance and first agricultural phase. When construction began the land surface supported snails which tolerated fairly dry, open grassland, with some scrub and woods. As work on the monument progressed the ecology seems to have been similar to the present chalk downland. Then, after the site was abandoned and

Knap Hill, a Neolithic causewayed enclosure, viewed from below Wansdyke

its ditches began to silt up, shade-loving snails returned, presumably to enjoy the scrub and woodland which was regenerating on the hillside and becoming thicker than before. Of the Neolithic builders' crops we know nothing, but judging from animal bones left on the site they used the downland for rearing far more cattle than sheep. Whatever their diet, the evidence from a middle-aged female skeleton found in a ditch showed that it had proved very bad indeed for her teeth.

We must set this meagre evidence from Pewsey Vale against information found elsewhere, especially around Avebury and Stonehenge. Current thinking reinforces our impression that piecemeal and sometimes temporary woodland clearance took place, aimed at winning land for pasture as well as crops; that grassland was not always well maintained, allowing scrub to return; and that primitive ploughing hastened soil erosion from the hillsides, whilst impoverishing soil and encouraging weeds. It is not until the centuries around 1,500 BC, the later Bronze Age, that we find evidence of more systematic and permanent mixed farming in and around the Vale of Pewsey; and now we may draw conclusions not only from pollen grains and tiny shells, but also from surviving field boundaries and ditches.

First there are ancient land surfaces buried under barrows. Analysis of soil beneath a barrow on Milton Hill revealed that woodland was cleared from the area before the barrow was built; at Red Shore near Adam's Grave a layer of ploughsoil containing a grain of cereal pollen was discovered in 1970 under a ploughed-out barrow. The existence of arable here on high downland suggests that either population pressure or deteriorating soil fertility in the valley had driven farmers to cultivate the margins. At Milton Hill quantities of animal bone left by the barrow builders were also uncovered; about half were from cattle, a quarter from pigs, and most of the rest sheep or goats. It was concluded that the animals formed part of a mixed arable and pastoral farming economy, of which the arable component had left no evidence.

Tangible remains of prehistoric arable farming show as small rectangular fields defined by low banks, which often cluster over several hundred hectares. In many respects they resemble the furlongs arranged in open fields which replaced them as the method of arable cultivation in the middle ages. Prehistoric field systems are only occasionally spectacular, but traces of many more have been detected by aerial photography; in Wiltshire they are nearly all on the chalk, and they survive best on slopes, where soil movement through ploughing has buttressed their banks. Although some have been proved to date from the Bronze Age, most dating evidence, if it exists, comes from later periods, and in the Iron Age and Romano-British periods they seem to have been the normal form of arable cultivation. Areas of field systems survive on the chalk downland on both sides of the Vale, especially north of Bishop's Cannings and Allington, and south of Wilsford and Charlton. Had William Cobbett turned his back momentarily on the 'land of promise' and looked behind him, he would have seen a well-preserved field system on Fyfield Down, a stone's throw away.

Because we generally see these field systems high up on the downland, we may imagine that these thin, unrewarding soils alone were worked by prehistoric ploughmen. It is far more likely, however, that similar fields once existed on the more fertile valley sides and well-drained areas of the valley floor, but that they have been almost entirely obliterated by later cultivation superimposed on them. Traces of such a system, with unusually small fields, have in fact been identified north of Picked Hill in Wilcot, and there may be another south of Rybury on the slopes above All Cannings. But what we are seeing on the downland are marginal lands pressed into service sporadically during times of shortage, and then left high and dry in remote places to survive unmolested to the present day.

Like their successors the medieval open fields, prehistoric and Roman field systems formed part of a mixed farming economy, and the rearing of cattle and sheep to enrich the soil with their manure was essential to the whole regime. Large numbers of animal bones recovered from archaeological sites, such as the important Iron Age settlement at All Cannings Cross, are one indication of this; another is the occurrence of long ditches, sometimes running for several kilometres across the downs, which were probably built to confine stock within certain areas. Some of these ranch boundaries seem to form part of adjacent field systems (for example on Wilsford and Allington Downs); others cut across field systems which had presumably gone out of use. Two ranch boundaries on the plain above Charlton, Wilsford and Rushall can each be traced for about 5km.

One further type of archaeological site, banked or ditched enclosures of various shapes and sizes, which are quite common in this area, may have served as useful pennings for sheep and cattle, even if this was not their principal function. A group of four circular ditches has been identified along the top of the escarpment south of Pewsey.

Martinsell from the east; a prehistoric hillfort commands its summit

Each encloses about 1-2ha, they are of Iron Age or Romano-British date, and seem to be associated with linear ditches and field systems. Hillforts are much larger Iron Age enclosures, often with defence as their primary aim, but it is highly likely that some had other functions as well, including perhaps enclosing stock. The recent archaeological interest in the prehistoric landscape around Marden Henge has identified vestiges of many more of these enclosures as cropmarks visible from the air.

It is unfortunate that our knowledge of prehistoric farming in the area comes almost entirely from the downland on either side of the Vale, because it is here, by the nature of the soil and the terrain, that agriculture can have been least successful. So we cannot explore in detail how Cobbett's three types of land – downland, hillside and valley floor – interacted to produce a viable farming economy for the prehistoric and Romano-British inhabitants of the Vale. Nor do we know for how long it continued. Recent work elsewhere suggests that the fundamental change occurred in the middle or later Saxon period. Certainly when we pick up the story again with the Saxons, we have a range of different evidence to consider.

For nine Pewsey Vale communities documents, purporting to date from the 9th or 10th century, have survived which describe, landmark by landmark, their territorial boundaries. Many landmarks are natural features, such as hills and streams; others are manmade, such as boundary stones, prehistoric barrows and buildings; yet others refer to isolated bushes, trees and tree-stumps. We shall see in the next chapter how these Saxon charters often describe boundaries drawn centuries earlier, which were to remain unaltered until the 19th century, and often right up to the present day. They stand as a kind of bridge, leading us back to the prehistoric world of field systems and ranch boundaries, and forward to the fully developed medieval pattern of open fields, and sheep-and-corn husbandry.

A number of the Vale's parish boundaries conform to a particular pattern. On the adjacent downland they are relatively straight, sometimes following old tracks or the linear ditches which we described above. But when they descend the hillside into the Vale itself they begin a series of right-angled turns for no obvious reason. Among many examples, we may cite the boundaries between West and Market Lavington, and between Manningford and Pewsey (both on the southern

escarpment); and between Bishop's and All Cannings, Stanton St Bernard
and Alton, and around Clench between Milton Lilbourne and Wootton
Rivers (all on the northern escarpment). This anomaly is best explained
by imagining that when the boundaries were drawn they crossed working
prehistoric or Roman field systems on the hillsides, and so by their
twists and turns have preserved vestiges of the old husbandry, which
was subsequently adapted to the open field arrangement which followed.
Saxon charters describe two of the boundaries cited above, and some of
the wording repays attention.

Stanton St Bernard's bounds, probably by then many centuries
old, were set down in 905. One downland landmark is the *hlinc reave*,
which perhaps means 'straight bank', and may refer to a ranch boundary;
another, which survives some 500m north of the Alton white horse, is
oxna mere, 'the oxen's pond', which indicates that then, as now, cattle

*The Saxon boundary of Stanton St Bernard descends the hillside and zigzags between
the prairie fields heading for the white building (the Barge Inn) in front of the distant
woodland. This view is taken from the Alton white horse, seen in the foreground, and
the Salisbury Plain escarpment forms the distant southern horizon (see also page 34).*

were pastured on these downs; and a third, as the boundary zigzags down the hill, is the *midmestan hrycg*, 'the middle ridge (of several)'. On the downland south of Pewsey, near the promontory with the quaint name of Denny Sutton Hipend, are several landmarks preserved in a charter of 987 which describe open field agriculture at work. There is a green *hlinc* (here probably a baulk between furlongs), a small *æcer* and another *æcer* (strips in a furlong), a 'long piece of projecting ploughland', and an 'old allotment of land at the boundary' (the word for allotment, *dola*, refers to an individual's share in an open field system). But, as at Stanton, the boundary elsewhere harks back to old ditches and a linear bank (*hlincrewe*) left over from the prehistoric and Roman system.

Landmarks in other charters help to fill out our picture of the emerging open-field system. On the Pewsey boundary near Kepnal in 940 the headlands (or plough-turning places) of strips were marked out by stakes; in 825 there were fifteen strips of arable next to the Alton–Pewsey road at Tawsmead, and Tawsmead itself probably means, 'the meadow in common or general use'; near Red Shore on the downs behind Adam's Grave there was a *gemænan garan*, which probably refers to a triangular plot of common field; and another gore, or triangle, which is recorded in 892, survives in the name Gores, a hamlet near Woodborough. Several charters refer to baulks and headlands, and we learn something too of other farming activities. There was a sheepwash, probably at Alton Priors, and a dairy farm in a clearing nearby; above Rainscombe was a path for oxen, and we have already found the oxen pond on Milk Hill. Groves (managed woods) are mentioned, as well as clearings, heath, brushwood and waste or marsh – perhaps indications that a period of neglect came between the breakdown of the old system and the adoption of the new.

Most present-day place names, in the Vale as elsewhere, are derived from Saxon words, and were probably coming into use during the period of transition depicted in the charters. Some confirm the impression of neglect, such as Wedhampton, 'the weed-infested farm', Bremhill (near Honeystreet), 'the bramble hill', and three Hatfields (at Stert, Beechingstoke and Oare), which refer to open heathland. Others describe woodland, and the inroads made by Saxon clearance – Woodborough and Wootton Rivers, of course, and most of the places which end in -leigh or -ley ('a glade or clearing in a wood, or the wood itself'), especially at the eastern end of the Vale towards Savernake. A few names seem to refer to land division: Flitwick near Wootton Rivers means 'dairy farm in disputed ownership', and Etchilhampton is 'the farmstead added on' – probably to All Cannings; land measurement is implied in the concept of a five-hide unit, which underlies the names Fiddington and Fyfield.

Saxon charters and names allow us to glimpse the transition from one mixed farming economy to another. The medieval system of large open fields divided into smaller blocks, known as furlongs, which consisted of strips (acres or lands) allotted to individuals, with crop rotation and common grazing controlled by the landowner through manorial courts, continued from the later Saxon period until the 19th century in many places, and the last remnant of strip cultivation survived at Stert until 1928. During the middle ages inquiries were often held to establish inheritance when a landowner died, and these

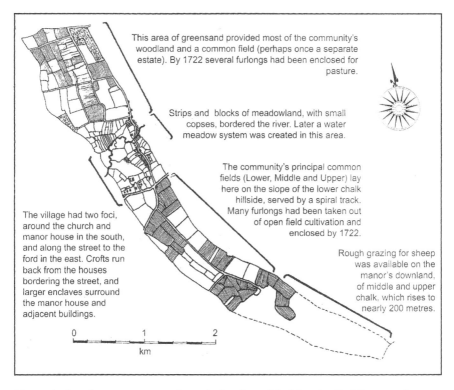

This area of greensand provided most of the community's woodland and a common field (perhaps once a separate estate). By 1722 several furlongs had been enclosed for pasture.

Strips and blocks of meadowland, with small copses, bordered the river. Later a water meadow system was created in this area.

The community's principal common fields (Lower, Middle and Upper) lay here on the slope of the lower chalk hillside, served by a spiral track. Many furlongs had been taken out of open field cultivation and enclosed by 1722.

The village had two foci, around the church and manor house in the south, and along the street to the ford in the east. Crofts run back from the houses bordering the street, and larger enclaves surround the manor house and adjacent buildings.

Rough grazing for sheep was available on the manor's downland, of middle and upper chalk, which rises to nearly 200 metres.

The agricultural arrangements of a typical strip parish, Manningford Bruce, redrawn from an estate map dated 1722 (WSA 1553/106)

sometimes describe the agricultural arrangements on the deceased's land. From these we can build up some picture of life and work on Pewsey Vale manors between about 1250 and 1350, when population and food requirements were probably at their peak.

Arable farming generally followed a two-field rotation, seen at its simplest in the East and West Fields at Fiddington and Chirton, and North and South Fields at Rushall. The rotation did not necessarily depend on the number of fields; Etchilhampton had only one field, whereas North Newnton and Woodborough probably had three or four. Nor was all arable equal in value: at Milton Lilbourne about two-thirds were worth 6d per acre, and one-third only 1d; on the lord's farm at Market Lavington 88 acres of sandy land were worth 3d each, 20 acres of 'deep' land were worth 8d, but 374 poor acres on the hill were only worth 2d each; Allington, however, with its land on the northern escarpment, boasted a large expanse of much better arable, reckoned at 10d per acre. By comparison the small acreages of precious meadow land possessed by each community, generally on the rich alluvium of the valley floor, might be worth as much as 24d or even 36d per acre, and their value to landowners might be enhanced by enclosing portions for their exclusive use; when he died in 1361 Thomas de Alden had enclosed three of his twelve acres of meadow at Manningford Bohun, and increased their value from 18d to 30d.

Cattle, for motive power, meat and milk, formed a part of this agricultural regime (Thomas de Alden had a herd of 80 'great cattle'), but sheep were more important. Their principal value lay in manuring the arable to maintain its fertility, but their wool and meat brought in useful additional wealth for both landlords and tenants. Landlords' flocks of 400 or more were not uncommon, and tenants collectively might own similar numbers. At Fiddington in 1309, for instance, the tenantry were permitted a maximum of 300, of which about half belonged to three individuals.

The tenants paid for their holdings in two ways: they performed services (or renders) to the lord, such as supplying labour for his land; and they paid rents and dues, both in money and in produce. At Easterton in 1258, for example, the tenants had to cart their lord's hay and corn, and take his corn to market. At nearby Fiddington fifty years later an elaborate code of services and payments had been worked out, covering poultry, threshing, mowing, carrying hurdles, selling horses, wax, washing sheep – everything, in fact, right down to the time and ingredients of the meal which the lord had to provide on a certain day: bread and ale, with a dish of meat or peas, at the ninth hour.

The open-field system, although it lasted in places for nearly a millennium, was never static. Fiddington's detailed regulations were probably imposed to increase efficiency at a time when a growing population demanded higher food production. To tackle the same problem marginal land was once again brought into cultivation, either by clearing woodland (this was known as assarting), or by forming cultivation terraces (strip lynchets) along the contours of steep hillsides. Assarting is recorded at Rainscombe in 1246, and in the Milton Lilbourne, Wootton Rivers and Martinsell areas after 1302. Strip lynchets may still be seen on many hillsides overlooking the Vale: above Charlton and West Lavington on the southern escarpment, for example; and along the great sweep of downland behind Bishop's Cannings and Allington on the north. Excavations in 1957-8 showed that a particularly fine flight of lynchets above Horton had buried an earlier field system of prehistoric type. The lynchets, here as elsewhere, were probably medieval.

Use of marginal land ebbed and flowed, as did the fortunes of landowners and tenants. But the basic structure of open-field agriculture in chalkland valleys remained largely intact. If we move forward from

Strip lynchets at Ram's Cliff on the southern escarpment near West Lavington

the 14th to the 17th century we find, at Milton Lilbourne for example, that there were still basically two fields, east and west, extending up the hillside, but by now they were divided according to soil quality, and designated East and West Sands Fields, East and West Clay Fields, and East and West Down Fields. A farmer who died there in 1627 held between 7 and 13 acres in each subdivision, as well as 6 horses, 12 cows and 160 sheep. The main differences from three centuries earlier, here as elsewhere, were that most valuable meadows and pasture grounds on the valley floor had by now been divided up into small closes for exclusive use, and that no longer did feudal lords farm their manors directly, requiring of their tenants services and payments in kind. Instead the manor farms were often leased, and the tenantry paid money rents, such as heriots and entry fines – kinds of inheritance tax – controlled and recorded by the manorial courts.

The landowners themselves employed agents to supervise the lessees and tenants. Such a man was Michael Woodward, who visited

The pond at Jones's Mill, Pewsey, an area of former water meadows now managed as a nature reserve

Stert and Alton Barnes each summer between 1659 and 1675, in his capacity as Warden of New College, Oxford, the manorial owner. His notebooks record an entertaining picture of a conscientious but strict taskmaster pitted against a resentful, surly and sometimes delinquent tenantry. At Stert in 1660 he requested that a terrier (or survey) of the manor farm be drawn up; it has survived, and reveals a holding of 80 acres of open arable land, 80 acres of sheep pasture, 9 closes of pasture and meadowland totalling 84 acres, and an 8-acre coppice wood. Unusually Stert's territory includes no downland, and the sheep, so necessary to enrich the arable, were grazed on low-lying clay pasture at Hatfield. By contrast another survey, of Lord Pembroke's manor of Stanton St Bernard, made in 1631, reveals that here there were sufficient downland and rough grazing to carry 2,500 sheep and about 150 cattle. Nearly 1,000 acres of arable open fields were farmed, by a freeholder, a lessee, and 18 copyholders or tenants. The freeholder and lessee had nearly half the arable and sheep between them; the average tenant farmed about 40 acres, owned some 80 sheep and a few cows, and held about 5 closes of meadow and pasture.

The Vale of Pewsey was a fertile, sturdy farming country long before Cobbett described it as his land of promise. Another eye witness, travelling from Pewsey to Devizes in about 1540, called it, 'playne champine [open] ground, frutfull of grasse and corne, especially good whete and barley'. This fruitfulness could be further enhanced by even more sheep, and during the 17th century efforts were made to increase the number of sheep which could be overwintered by stimulating earlier and better meadow grass. The 'floating' of water meadows was the first of many stratagems designed to revolutionize agriculture –innovations which in time would lead to the demise of the traditional farming regime.

Floating involved damming and diverting a river so that its flow, from about November to March, could be channelled across the whole meadow, as a shallow, ever-moving sheet of silty water. This enriched the soil and kept the meadow from freezing, so that grass grew earlier and more vigorously. Sheep could graze these water meadows in early spring, and later a bumper hay crop could be taken. Water meadows worked best where a strong, reliable head of water was available, such as along the lower reaches of the Wiltshire chalk rivers; but they were also constructed in the Vale of Pewsey. Indeed, three years after the 1631

Stanton survey, the tenants were ordered to scour the ditches of what were probably recent water meadows. Many Pewsey Vale communities maintained water meadows in the 18th and 19th centuries, including Marden, Wilsford, Rushall and Manningford Bruce. At Charlton new meadows were floated between 1781 and 1783, and remains of the system survive west of the village; and at Hare Street, between Wilcot and Manningford, traces of the ridges, carriers and drains of a water meadow system were still visible in 2005. The best example of former water meadows publicly accessible and surviving, although obscured by later land use, is at Jones's Mill, north of Pewsey. Here the infant Avon's water supply had to be augmented from springs, especially after the thirsty canal was built nearby in 1809. During the 19th century drowning ceased (as the controlled flooding was known), and ponds were later made for watercress; since 1980 these meadows, with their fenland habitat of marsh-loving plants – including valerian and meadowsweet, alder and willow, sedges and devil's bit scabious – have been managed as a county nature reserve.

Of course water meadows are not the only special use to which land in the Vale has been put, nor has sheep-and-corn husbandry been the sole economic concern. A charter of 940 mentions a 'woad-clearing' near Rainscombe, and Domesday Book tells us about 'a good vineyard' at Wilcot in 1086 – clearly a civilized place, since it also boasted a new church and an excellent house. All the Vale north and east of Knap Hill, Pewsey and Easton Royal fell within the designated area of Savernake Forest during the 12th and 13th centuries, not because it was dense woodland, but to prevent any farming or other activities which might jeopardise the king's hunting. Nevertheless there were and are small woods in the Vale, essential for fuel and building materials, attached to most communities, and often in steep or remote places, or on poor and difficult land.

Apart from the bishop of Salisbury's deer park at Potterne, no medieval owner emparked land in the Vale, but later landlords were more ruthless in modifying portions of the landscape. Admiral Montagu's seat at Stowell Lodge, near Wilcot, and Edward Poore's at Rushall, both disrupted farmland and settlements. A 17th-century example of garden or parkland landscaping, described and praised both by Warden Woodward (who visited it in 1673 between business at Stert and Alton), and by the antiquary John Aubrey, lay in the valley beside West Lavington, and its southward continuation is familiar to observant Salisbury-bound travellers on the A360 (see Walk 5). The best formal gardens now to be enjoyed in the Vale are probably those at Conock Manor (of 1765-1820, mostly after 1817) and Oare House (1921-5 and later).

Gardening on a commercial scale also has been possible on some of the better-drained greensand soils. Aubrey enthused over the turnips grown at Burbage: 'They are the best that ever I did eate, and are sent for far and neere; they are not tough and stringy like other turnips, but cutt like marmalad.' At the other end of the Vale in the 19th century and later an extensive area of greensand north of Easterton and Market Lavington has been devoted to market gardening and fruit-growing; much of its produce found its way into the Easterton jam factory, which was established first in 1868 and continued until closure in 1988 and demolition in 2014.

An overgrown lake in the landscaped coombe at the Warren, above West Lavington

But back to farming, and to the agricultural revolution of which water meadows were the harbinger. An official report, published in 1794 and revised in 1811, praised Wiltshire's water meadows, but attacked the retention of open-field agriculture as hindering progress. The system, it conceded, was in part dictated by the long, narrow parishes, so that the benefits of enclosure would be less marked here than elsewhere; but the advantages – financial savings, convenience, independence, and the chance to innovate – would nevertheless outweigh any prejudices and difficulties. By 1794, in fact, the formal enclosure of the Vale of Pewsey was well under way. Parts of Pewsey, Charlton, Coate, Market Lavington, Patney and Milton Lilbourne had all been enclosed by act of Parliament between 1777 and 1781; acts for eleven more parishes or tithings went through up to 1811, and the same number between 1811 and 1842. Many of the later acts merely tidied up earlier enclosures made by

Whatley's foundry speciaslised in pumps and other agricultural machinery, and their building now houses the Pewsey Heritage Centre. The business survives elsewhere.

private agreement, and similar agreements were made in parishes not touched by formal legislation. Thus within some 60 years open-field agriculture, the second great era of farming in the Vale, had been all but extinguished. A third era, with its manifold social and ecological consequences, had begun.

So many changes have occurred since 1800 that only the briefest outline can be given here. Freedom to experiment led farmers to introduce more elaborate rotations, and to try new crops – such as flax, which was grown at Horton during the 1850s. Large tracts of downland (above Allington, All Cannings, Rushall and Upavon, for example) were converted to wheat and barley cultivation, initially by 'burnbaking' (paring off and burning the turf), and then maintained by careful management and artificial fertilizers. The traditional breed of sheep, the Wiltshire horn, was allowed to disappear, and was replaced by Merino, Southdown and Hampshire Down breeds in turn. Machinery was introduced, especially from the 1820s, and the hated portable threshing machine provoked a violent protest from farm labourers. In November 1830 fires were started and machines destroyed at Wilcot, Oare, Stanton St Bernard, All Cannings and elsewhere. Maria Hare, whom we met on Adam's Grave, was herself a terrified witness when her neighbour at Alton Barnes, a large farmer, was attacked and injured. But the march of machinery was relentless, and during the 19th century small agricultural engineering factories operated in Pewsey and Market Lavington. A breed of large businessmen farmers emerged who were enthusiastic mechanizers. Such was Arthur Stratton, who farmed 3,000 acres in and around Alton Priors, owned six sets of double steam ploughing tackle, and was vice-chairman of a national organisation, the Steam Plough Development Association. Paradoxically, he met a premature end in 1918 when run over by a steam train at Woodborough Station.

Arthur Stratton came from one of several farming dynasties which emerged in the Vale during the 19th century. The Browns of Horton, the Ferrises of Milton Lilbourne and Manningford, and especially the Strattons of Woodborough and elsewhere, spearheaded farming consolidation and innovation. When crop production slumped after 1880 in the wake of poor harvests and foreign competition Frank Stratton began to buy up holdings at depressed prices, and turned them into dairy farms supplying liquid milk by train to London consumers. Farms at

Tombs of members of the Stratton farming dynasty in Woodborough churchyard

Manningford, Rushall. Charlton, Horton and Patney became part of his company's empire, which for a time controlled the largest acreage of any farming concern in England. Dairying was accompanied by modest but far-reaching innovations – piped water to remote areas, and barbed wire fences – which appeared alongside an increasing use of steam, and later motor and electrical power, and greater reliance on artificial fertilizers and pesticides. Another major change occurred between 1897 and 1899 when virtually all the Salisbury Plain downland extending back from the Vale's southern escarpment between the Lavingtons and Upavon was acquired by the War Department for military training. Limited farming activity was possible in certain areas – 500 cattle and 5,000 sheep were grazed from Urchfont Hill Farm between the wars – but much of this wilderness has been used for target practice by more than a hundred years of artillery, and is littered with unexploded mortars.

Milk production was the principal farming activity in the area before and between the wars. A survey published in 1940 described the greensand vale as, 'largely pastoral, with arable fields scattered

We'll keep the red flag flying here. The army vedette post on Redhorn Hill, above Urch-font, barring access to the former downland rough pastures of Pewsey Vale farmers.

throughout, except for more marked concentrations of arable land around Woodborough, Burbage and North Newnton'. Wheat was the principal cereal, with oats, clover and fodder crops, but no barley. Dairy cattle reigned supreme, pigs and poultry were reared, but sheep were unimportant. The hillslopes retained some arable, but many of the large cornfields, especially on the southern escarpment, were divided up and fenced for pasture between 1925 and 1940. During the last 75 years machines and agrochemicals have further loosened the age-old bond between soil, settlements and agriculture, so that farming in the Vale, as elsewhere, can be dictated as much by market forces and government subsidies as by the tradition of mixed farming. In general, however, dairying is still the main enterprise on the greensand of the valley floor, much of which has been designated as grade one agricultural land (of exceptional quality); on the hillsides, which are largely grade two (high quality) land, good yields of wheat are achieved in huge unenclosed fields, and the arable side of the equation has returned to its pre-1880 importance.

The slopes above Alton are still farmed by descendants of the Strattons

Damaging though some of the agricultural practices of the last two centuries have been to a chalkland and valley ecology which evolved over millennia, the prognosis is healthier than forty years ago. The Pewsey Downs national nature reserve (see Walk 4) occupies 170ha of downland, extending along the northern escarpment from Tan Hill to Knap Hill, and embraces the familiar landmarks of Adam's Grave and the Alton white horse. Its herb-rich sward of red and sheep's fescue supports many rare chalkland plants, including various orchids, the round-headed rampion and the tuberous thistle. Like a vast impressionist canvas the summer hillside of dabs and swirls in yellow and purple on a shimmering green sea allows us to relive Cobbett's vision, and to experience what must have existed everywhere on chalkland Wiltshire three hundred years ago, when Aubrey wrote of 'romancy plaines and boscages', and 'turfe rich and fragrant with thyme and burnet'.

As well as its nature reserve, and its counterpart along the escarpment opposite, the Vale is home to one of the largest and most important attempts to reintroduce organic farming into British agriculture. Barry Wookey's land extended over much of the parishes of Rushall and Charlton, 670ha altogether. It was a mixed farm, with beef cattle, horses, and a breeding flock (in the mid-1980s) of 750 ewes, which was run as a separate enterprise; the principal crop was wheat, stoneground in the farm's own mill, but grass, kale and swedes were also grown for fodder. Gradually, field by field, between 1970 and 1985 the whole farm was converted to chemical-free cultivation. It achieved an international reputation, and was in the vanguard of the burgeoning organic farming movement. Wookey wrote about the project in a book, in which he described with Cobbett-like enthusiasm the rationale behind the techniques and processes which made up his farming year; an appendix listed 95 species of wild flower identified on his farm in 1984. His son Nigel extended the organic regime to land in Upavon parish, and completed the process by the end of the century; Rushall Organics in 2018 farmed almost 2,000ha, half as arable, and the rest as permanent grass, woods, or downland.

Bounds appointed between Alton Barnes (left of the bank) and Stanton St Bernard (right of the bank). They were set down in 905 AD but may be centuries earlier, since they ignore Wansdyke: see pages 19-20 and 38-9.

3
THE APPOINTED
BOUNDS

I N THE PREVIOUS chapter we attempted to plough a fairly straight furrow across several thousand years of agricultural history, without becoming distracted by the people, buildings and villages on either side of us. Their turn will come shortly. But first we must explore how and when the Vale was divided up into the territories and farming units – many of them present-day parishes – which throughout are serving as our examples. We have dropped a few hints about this already: Fyfield, the five-hide unit; long narrow parishes which the 1811 report saw as obstructing progress; and, of course, the Saxon boundary charters. What are we to make of it all?

From West Lavington to Burbage the Vale of Pewsey today is divided into 29 civil parishes, and between 1974 and 2009 (when Wiltshire became a unitary authority) they all lay in the administrative district of Kennet. At the beginning of the 19th century, when parishes were units of both religious and secular local government, there was one fewer; since then there have been repeated attempts to rationalize their boundaries, so that four of our modern parishes – Easterton, Etchilhampton, Roundway and Stert – have resulted from the breaking up of larger units, and two – Alton and Manningford – are combinations of smaller ancient parishes. Roundway lost its parochial status in 2017 because much of it had by then become suburban Devizes. Until 1858 Fullaway, a hamlet near Stert, lay outside the parochial system altogether, a kind of no-man's-land.

Parishes are usually considered to be the product of the late-Saxon and early-Norman centuries (as we shall see in Chapter 5), when a uniform system of religious taxation (tithes) was imposed, and it

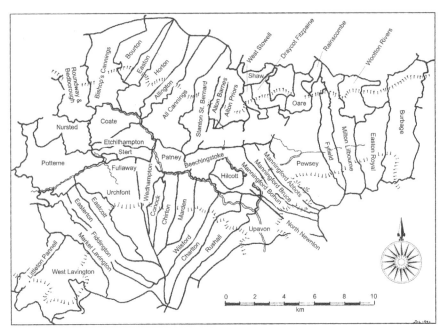

Tithings in the Vale of Pewsey

became important to know which land was paying for the support of which church. But behind and before the parish structure lay an earlier arrangement of estates, which to some extent survived the middle ages and could still be traced in the 19th century. They were known as tithings, and there were over fifty of them in Pewsey Vale. In fact their number fluctuated; some by the 19th century had lost their significance (Clench in Milton Lilbourne, for example), or had been combined (such as Bourton and Easton in Bishop's Cannings), whilst others were artificial creations of the middle ages (Yardland and Cosset in Urchfont). Many tithing boundaries, we must assume, were taken over by the medieval church and used to define parishes and dependent chapelries; hence the smaller parishes were not divided into tithings, or rather had been a single tithing which became a parish in its own right.

The name 'tithing' is related to 'tithe' and 'tenth', and shows that these territories were part of a decimal system of land division. The unit of measurement was the hide, a notional area of land sufficient to support an extended family or single farmstead. In theory ten hides made a tithing, and ten tithings made a hundred, which is the name given to the larger administrative unit which we shall encounter shortly.

It is necessary to add the qualification 'in theory', because although reckoning by hides seems to have taken place in much of England by the 7th century, it is not until Domesday Book in 1086 that the hidal assessments for most places are recorded, and by then centuries of chopping and changing had taken place. Nevertheless a look at Domesday Book reveals that a number of estates in Pewsey Vale were still reckoned at ten hides or thereabouts (Chirton, Conock, Etchilhampton, Woodborough, Manningford Abbots, Marden and West Lavington), and many more were expressed as multiples of ten hides (Stanton St Bernard and Alton Priors were 20, Urchfont, Wootton Rivers and Pewsey were 30 or thereabouts, Potterne was just under 60, and Bishop's Cannings was 70). Others were assessed at five hides (indeed the names of two – Fyfield and Fiddington – actually mean five hides, as we saw in the previous chapter), and still others can plausibly be combined to give round numbers (Allington and All Cannings together make 30, Rushall and Upavon make nearly 40, and so on). Hardly anywhere does not fit, or cannot easily be made to fit, into this scheme of fives, tens, and multiples of ten.

The numbers game is one of the signs that the Vale of Pewsey in Saxon times had been organised into a systematic division of land units, which has in many cases been perpetuated by our modern parish boundaries. Another indication is the shape and composition of these tithings. They are far from haphazard; in fact they reflect quite closely the geology and farming regime which we have already explored. Most consist of strips of land, sometimes no more than a few hundred metres wide, which extend from the valley floor, across the greensand pasture. the lower chalk cornland, and up the escarpment on to the rough downs. These strips may be nearly 10km long (such as Fiddington, Rushall and Milton Lilbourne), and many others are between 6km and 8km. This pattern occurs right along the Vale's southern escarpment, broken only by river gaps at Upavon and West Lavington; it may be seen, too, although slightly less regularly, along the northern escarpment, especially at the Cannings or western end. At Pewsey and Milton Lilbourne the Vale is narrow enough for territories to extend right across, and up on to the chalkland both north and south. Upavon straddles the Avon valley in the same way, as do a number of parishes further south.

There can be no doubt that the agricultural potential of the soils lies behind this arrangement. By these means each community had its share of wet meadows, greensand for rich pasture and root crops, better-drained chalk loam for its arable fields, a water supply from river or springs, rough grazing on the downs for cattle and sheep, and woodland scattered in steep and awkward places. That this was the intention is confirmed by looking at those few tithings which did not conform to the pattern. They lay on the valley floor, too far from either escarpment, landlocked, as it were, by neighbouring territories from a share of the chalk. But in fact four of them – Nursteed, Coate, Etchilhampton and Stert – contrived to share between them the chalk outlier of Etchilhampton Hill; all the others had a certain amount of chalk within their territories, though in Patney and Beechingstoke it was admittedly very small. Patney, however, seems from an early date to have been linked with Alton Priors, which had ample chalkland, and there were connections too between North Newnton and Wilcot (in the Vale), and Rainscombe and Oare (on the hill) respectively.

We have seen from the Saxon charters, which describe in detail the boundaries of some of these territories, that part at least of this system of tithings was in place by the 9th century, and we have said that division into hides may have taken place by the 7th century. One more consideration may enable us to push further back still the possible date for this land division in the area. Across the southern Marlborough Downs, just beyond the Vale's northern escarpment, runs a massive linear earthwork, the Wansdyke. Wansdyke was clearly built for defence,

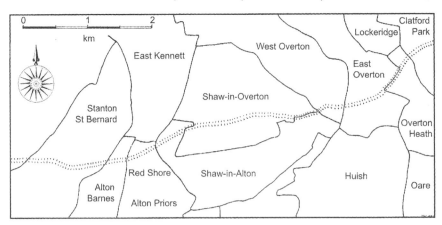

The relationship of part of Wansdyke to tithing and parish boundaries

and most (though not all) scholars regard it as a product of the 5th century, after the departure of Roman government. The earthwork is on such a scale that if the tithings had been laid out after its construction, we should expect them to have used it as a convenient boundary and landmark. In fact the tithing boundaries consistently ignored it. This is particularly noticeable around Red Shore, north of Adam's Grave. Here the tithings of Alton Barnes and Alton Priors (the latter recorded in a Saxon charter) terminated just a field's width north of Wansdyke; conversely Shaw and Huish, due east of Red Shore, extended to just short of Wansdyke (except in one place), while Stanton St Bernard to the west crossed Wansdyke and owned a small tract of downland, some 1km x 2km, to its north. Although it has been challenged, the most likely inference of these awkward disjunctions must be that the tithings were there first, and that Wansdyke came later.

Now if this is true, and if, as their regularity suggests, the tithings are a product of systematic land division by one or several powerful landowners, two conclusions follow first, that underlying the tithings were larger and older territories; and second, that already by the 5th century these older territories were being broken up. It is only a short step from here to the world of villa estates and small towns in the 4th century, when Roman power in Britain was beginning to lose its grip. In some parts of England this link between Roman estates and later boundaries can be clearly demonstrated. In the Vale of Pewsey, however, we have to restrict ourselves to a few observations and suggestions. And the starting point for these must be the hundreds, the groupings of (nominally) ten tithings or one hundred hides which formed one of the tiers of local government until the 19th century.

When they eventually ceased to have any administrative function, in 1894, the hundreds had probably undergone more than a millennium of piecemeal change and reorganisation. By the 19th century there were four hundreds involved in the Vale of Pewsey, called Potterne and Cannings, Elstub and Everleigh, Swanborough, and Kinwardstone. Elstub and Everleigh, to which Patney and Alton Priors belonged, may be discounted from our quest for early territories, as in its evolved form it was created for the convenience of the medieval bishops of Winchester, to embrace their scattered Wiltshire properties. Potterne and Cannings was a composite hundred, controlling land around Devizes

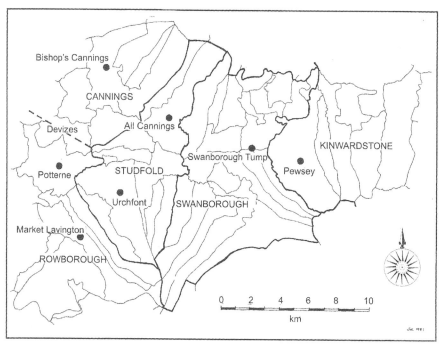

Hundreds in the Vale of Pewsey

at the western end of the Vale. It was formed in the middle ages out
of parts of two land units, one called Cannings, and the other (which
included Potterne) called Rowborough. At the time of Domesday Book
the tithings which made up the estate of Bishop's Cannings totalled
70 hides, and All Cannings and Allington together were assessed at
30 hides; here, therefore, we have the suggestion of a true hundred
of Cannings. Rowborough's constituents in the 11th century (chiefly
Potterne and the Lavingtons) totalled 96 hides, just short of the full
hundred. Kinwardstone, assessed in Domesday Book at 196 hides, was
really a double-hundred, and much of it lay east of the Vale of Pewsey,
centred on Great Bedwyn. But it included two 30-hide estates, Pewsey
and Wootton Rivers, which seem also to have embraced Fyfield, Milton
and Easton. The 19th-century hundred of Swanborough was very large
– including in fact most of the Vale – but this was because by then it had
swallowed up half of Rowborough and the whole of another hundred,
known as Studfold, which was centred on Urchfont. Swanborough itself
in the 11th century occupied the central block of Pewsey Vale, from
Stanton and Marden eastwards to the Manningfords, Wilcot and Oare.

It was assessed at 183 hides, so was nearly a double hundred, but had no natural centre, nor were any of its constituents particularly large, except the estate of roughly 40 hides at Rushall and Upavon.

It would be rash to suggest that the boundaries of these hundreds, even in their earliest recoverable guise at the end of the Saxon period, represent anything like the territories created during the Roman occupation (or indeed the tribal territories inherited by the Romans from prehistory), and bequeathed to their successors. They may however offer a few pointers as to where the important places – the estate centres – may have been in the late-Roman and early-Saxon periods, pointers which we can compare with evidence from archaeology, names and elsewhere.

At the western end of the Vale we may identify territories based on three places: the Cannings, Potterne, and the Lavingtons. Cannings is one of a class of similar place-names ending in -ingas, which are thought to represent quite an early stage in Saxon tribal organisation. It has been suggested that it may have been the successor to a large Roman territory, embracing much of the Vale and the Avebury area to the north, which subsequently divided into hundreds and later into the smaller tithings and parishes which we have described. Potterne was an early acquisition by Wessex bishops, and became an important ecclesiastical centre; a medieval deanery was named after it, and deaneries too are thought to be relics of earlier divisions. Lavington's importance at the

Tangible evidence of Potterne's early importance is this font, which bears around its rim an inscription in 10th-century or earlier lettering from the book of Psalms. It was probably installed in a forerunner of the present church which has been excavated nearby.

The 'Font' at Urchfont, a small lake fed by a spring used in the Roman period

beginning of Saxon colonisation was demonstrated in 1990 by the discovery of a large pagan Saxon cemetery and associated settlement very close to the site of a Roman building on Grove Farm near Market Lavington church. Moving eastwards the next hundred, Studfold, had its medieval meeting place next to the main road (the Lydeway) which runs close to Urchfont, its largest constituent. Urchfont itself, and Wickham Green nearby, both have names which are thought to have been coined by the Saxons to describe a Roman settlement continuing in use during the Dark Ages. The group of tithings at the eastern end of the Vale was perhaps controlled from Pewsey, where another substantial early Saxon cemetery was discovered and excavated between 1969 and 1972. Although no settlement associated with the cemetery was discovered, it is likely to have been situated nearby. Swanborough hundred took its name from a prehistoric barrow, Swanborough Tump, where the hundred courts met; it lies in a remote spot on the valley floor, equidistant from Woodborough, Wilcot and Manningford, and with no important Roman or Saxon settlement known to have existed nearby. If, however, Swanborough was really a double hundred, we should perhaps be

Swanborough Tump, a flattened prehistoric barrow used as the hundred meeting place

looking for two estate centres, extending up the northern and southern escarpments respectively. Where they might have been is guesswork, but for what it is worth we may note that Roman villa complexes are known to have existed at Stanchester, near West Stowell, and close to the site of Manningford Bruce church. Swanborough Tump lies between them, about 2km from each.

Arguments and suggestions of this kind are somewhat speculative, of course, and since the 1970s there has been prolonged and continuing academic debate about the antiquity of specific boundaries and boundaries in general. Scholarly opinion has become polarised over whether or not late-Saxon boundaries can be used to tell us anything at all about Roman territorial organisation, and how and when it broke down. But whether prehistoric, Roman or late-Saxon, the point to be made is that the boundaries of the Vale are great survivors, often far older than the villages, buildings and farms whose lands they now define. Our next task will be to look at the development of settlements within these appointed bounds.

Urchfont,one of the more successful and populous villages in the Vale, and justifiably celebrated as one of the most attractive

4
WINNERS AND
LOSERS

THE VILLAGE STREET became a cul-de-sac, which led first to the church, and then to a large farm complex beyond. I parked by the churchyard wall, as the sign instructed. A gravel drive ran to the former rectory, opposite a timber-framed cottage by the church path. I walked back up the street, past playground swings on the green next to a slate-roofed 19th-century school, and on to the shop – a Spar, with Calor Gas and post box. Opposite, the 'best-kept village' plaques were displayed above the notice board next to the door of the village hall. And so up the street, which in places has settled to shoulder height below its bordering gardens, past brick cottages, more substantial timber-framed houses under thatch, modern bungalows and offset council houses, mostly now privately owned. Leading from the street were lanes and drives, running back beside half-hidden cottages to a footpath along the ends of the gardens. A man walking his dog nodded, and a tractor passed. Another small village green, triangular, with newish seat and litter bin, and then the street became a cul-de-sac again, called Townsend, and closed by a view of the downs beyond. House names – the Old Forge, Cross Keys House – signified earlier functions. Further on were new houses along an unobtrusive close. Woodsmoke after rain, birdsong and the cawing of rooks in a clump of high trees, lunchtime and no-one about.

Even readers familiar with the Vale from childhood might waver at this description of a walk (which I made in 1990). Easton Royal perhaps, or Chirton, or maybe Wilsford. Actually, it was All Cannings. The poet Edward Thomas voiced the same difficulty:

To turn back then and seek him, where was the use?
There were three Manningfords, – Abbots, Bohun, and Bruce;
And whether Alton, not Manningford, it was
My memory could not decide, because
There was both Alton Barnes and Alton Priors.
All had their churches, graveyards, farms and byres,
Lurking to one side up the paths and lanes,
Seldom well seen except by aeroplanes. . .

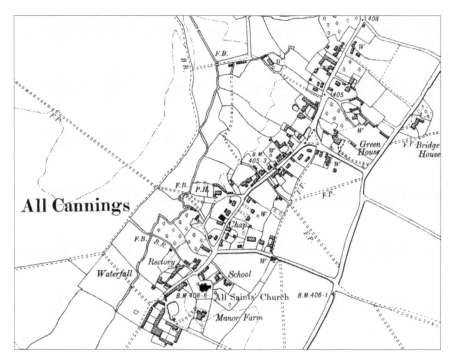

All Cannings village, as mapped by the Ordnance Survey in 1899

The view from an aeroplane, or more conveniently from a map, enables us to gauge the similarities and differences of village plans in the Vale of Pewsey. All Cannings is typical in its arrangement along either side of a fairly straight village street; about twenty villages and hamlets in the Vale share this feature. Some streets, such as those of Burbage, Easton Royal, Hilcott, Littleton Pannell and Oare, are portions of present or former main roads, and so the position and alignment of these villages may have been dictated by already-existing routes. But most, in Thomas's phrase, 'lurk to one side', and are not major highways. At All Cannings well-defined straight rear boundaries run parallel to the street behind back gardens on each side, and are followed in places by footpaths. This too is characteristic of many villages; it can be well seen, for example, at Coate, Chirton, Etchilhampton and Wootton Rivers, among others, and tends to show through more clearly on Victorian maps, before modern infilling and estate-building obscured it. Such regularity, which results in blocks of rectangular gardens or tenements, must be the product of deliberate village planning, and is usually assigned to the early middle ages.

The position of the church and churchyard in relation to these planned streets is worth noticing. At All Cannings, as we saw, they lie at one end of the street, next to the principal farmhouse. Easton Royal (an Elizabethan church on the site of its medieval predecessor) and Stert

At Rushall the church stands deserted in parkland near the river, but the mound next to it (beside the telegraph pole) conceals the buried remains of the manor house which was demolished in 1840. Its owner had transplanted the villagers to cottages out of sight in order to create his park.

(a chapel-of-ease) occupy similar positions, and at Wootton Rivers the church is set back from the linear street plan, abutting the courtyard of the manor house. A similar juxtaposition of church and manor house occurs in some villages without the linear planned element, for example Manningford Abbots and Alton Barnes. At two places, Wilcot and Stert, the churches were damaged by fire because of their proximity to their manor houses. Even where the church and present manor house stand apart, the church often abuts a farmyard (at Stanton St Bernard, for example) or the site of a vanished manor house (as at Rushall), or seems to form part of an irregular village nucleus which is linked to, but probably not an integral part of, the linear plan. This may be the case at All Cannings, and is well seen at Chirton, where the straight street turns abruptly by the churchyard; at its neighbour, Marden, the church and its surrounding cluster of buildings are likewise set apart from the straight village street further south.

Many of the settlements of Pewsey Vale have, or had, an open area, which we may call a village green. Some, like All Cannings, and also Wilsford and Urchfont, seem to have had two greens, one at each end of their streets. At their simplest these greens were no more than a triangular area where roads joined, a slightly enlarged T-junction, and to envisage them now we must in some cases mentally strip away the tarmac to reveal the grass and mud of earlier generations. Small greens of this kind exist at Beechingstoke and Patney, at the west end of Wilsford, the north end of Easton Royal (crossed by the main road) and probably at Milton Lilbourne, where Havering Lane meets the village street. In at least two cases – Chirton and Marden – the street itself was formerly much wider, and so made a long rectangular green (a surviving local example of this plan is at Poulshot, west of Devizes). Chirton still has something of this flavour near the school, but at Marden successive encroachments during the 19th century have reduced the formerly wide green to the width of a normal village street.

Encroachment, of an informal, piecemeal, and often illegal nature, was a frequent and widespread occurrence, at least since the 17th century. Cottages appeared haphazardly around greens, along the edges of common land or waste, and beside roads and tracks. Areas of this so-called 'squatter' development may be identified on the edges of many Pewsey Vale villages, sometimes with the characteristic name

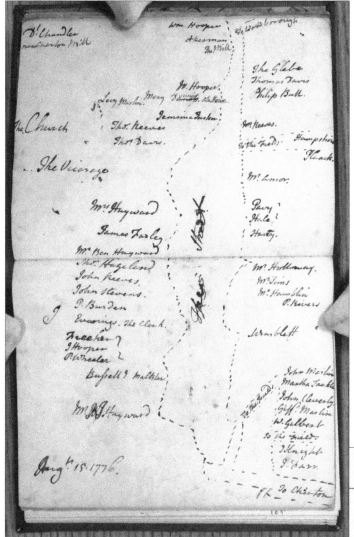

This sketch map of Marden green made in 1776 (WSA 510/11) can be compared with the Ordnance Survey map of 1899. At the earlier date the green is wide and has about forty householders living around it; by the later date the process of turning it into a village street is well under way.

Townsend, which we discovered at All Cannings. At Wedhampton, a seldom-visited hamlet near Urchfont, there is a good example. Here a linear street of large houses and farms runs northwards from the main road, and eventually forks; the resulting triangular green is flanked and encroached upon by humbler, higgledy-piggledy cottages. Burbage has such settlements at both ends of its linear street – Stibb Green, at the northern end, is a typical triangle, whereas the straggling commons near Seymour Pond at the southern end have just the occasional randomly sited cottage and smallholding. At Charlton a colony of wasteland cottages along White's Lane, west of the village, was demolished during the 19th century.

Two points should be made about what we have noticed so far. First, Pewsey Vale is a region where villages are the usual form of settlement. There are no large towns, only two industrial hamlets (Honeystreet and New Mill), and not really (except perhaps at its eastern and western edges) any areas of scattered farmsteads away from the village nucleus. True, there are plenty of settlements which may be regarded as too small to call villages. Hamlets of this kind may merely be outlying farmsteads such as are commonly found where villages predominate (East Sharcott, Knowle and Southcott, all around Pewsey, are typical examples), but in many cases, as we shall see, present-day hamlets were once larger and more important. And this leads to the second point: the Vale's landscape of villages is not static, but dynamic. Settlements may be enlarged – by a planned medieval street, for example, a 17th-century squatter enclave, or a modern housing estate – or they may never develop beyond a cluster of cottages and farm buildings. Two settlements may grow together (such as West Lavington and Littleton Pannell, or Eastcott and Easterton), or there may be movement from one focus to another (from North Newnton to Hilcott, or East Stowell to Wilcot Green). Places may go into decline or disappear altogether. Slowly, imperceptibly sometimes, the scene changes, like clouds in a windless sky.

The rise and fall of settlements are closely linked to their wealth and population, and it is fortunate that data about these survive from the middle ages onwards. Excluding Potterne, Bishop's Cannings, Alton Priors and Burbage (for which some totals are defective or problematical) the adult population of the Vale in 1377 was roughly 3,000, and in 1676

Pewsey's modest growth during the 18th century is reflected in its High Street

it had doubled to about 6,000. We may estimate that there were at this later date 3-4,000 children, giving a total population of between 9,000 and 10,000. This compares with total populations for the same area of 11,000 in 1811, 10,600 in 1911, and 14,400 in 1991. In other words, considerable expansion took place between 1377 and 1676, followed by virtual stagnation, which has continued until recently. But within this overall picture the fortunes of individual settlements have been very varied. Between 1377 and 1676, for instance, Market Lavington and Huish did indeed double their populations, reflecting the overall trend, but at three neighbouring communities at the eastern end of the Vale, Milton Lilbourne, Easton Royal and Wootton Rivers, and also at Woodborough, the population more than trebled; conversely Patney and Wilcot actually declined in numbers, and several other places – Beechingstoke, Charlton and Wilsford, for example – returned only modest growth.

Between 1676 and 1811, when the overall population probably grew by little more than 10%, similar variations occurred. Rushall and Marden declined significantly, whereas there was substantial growth in the Lavingtons, and in an area bounded by Stanton St Bernard, Wilcot and the Manningfords. During the 19th century when, against the national trend of an unprecedented population explosion, Pewsey Vale actually declined slightly, only in Pewsey itself was there marked growth. The Vale was not unusual among rural areas in this respect, as impoverished labourers sought their fortunes in the new industrial conurbations or overseas. One positive consequence of this diaspora was that the Vale has become celebrated in Australia, where 1839 émigré Joseph Gilbert (from Puckshipton) decided in 1847 to name his new vineyard after his homeland, and founded the Pewsey Vale winery still renowned for its Riesling.

The modest rise of Pewsey before 1900 continued through the 20th century, and was paralleled at Market Lavington, Burbage and Upavon. In general terms the larger communities have grown larger, and the smaller have remained static or become smaller still. By 2011, with extensive new housing estates and a parish total of 4,679, Pewsey is the most populous community in the Vale and is continuing to grow rapidly. Market Lavington, at 2,213 in 2011, is therefore less than half Pewsey's size in population terms.

Alongside the census data we may place other figures derived from taxation returns, and compare them with the villages as we see them now. All Cannings, for example, with its satellite communities of Allington, Etchilhampton and perhaps Fullaway, together accounted

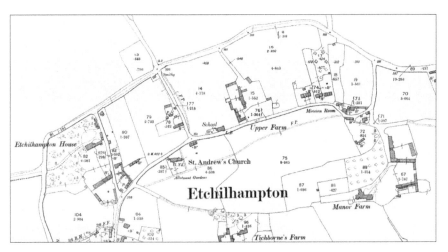

By 1899, when this Ordnance Survey map was revised, Etchilhampton was fragmenting, with gaps along its village street. The through route for traffic had transferred to its former back lane, curving around the north of the village, and houses were concentrated west of the church and north of Manor Farm. During the 20th century the village street atrophied into a footpath.

in 1332 for nearly 12% of the total wealth of Pewsey Vale (excluding once again Potterne, Bishop's Cannings, Alton Priors and Burbage), and over 11% of its population in 1377. But then its share began to decline – under 10% in 1576, under 9% in 1676, under 8% in 1811, barely 6% in 1911, and under 5% in 1981. This decline is reflected in the shrinkage of the four settlements. At Etchilhampton so many houses have been lost that the village has broken into two halves, an east end around Manor Farm, and a west end around the church (see Walk 2). Settlement earthworks east of Manor Farm show that the medieval village extended a considerable distance beyond its present eastern limit. Allington, likewise, preserves the empty crofts and surface irregularities characteristic of a shrunken settlement, and at Fullaway (which was never very large) the community has dwindled to a single farm. All Cannings itself has lost houses around the larger of its two greens, and possibly also south of the church and Manor Farm.

The neighbouring territory of Bishop's Cannings, for which no 1676 population figure was recorded, presents a similar picture of depopulation. At first glance it seems to be an example of the dispersed settlement pattern commonly found on the west Wiltshire claylands; indeed, a native described how: 'There was no concentration of houses in any particular place; they just gathered in little groups along the roads and by-lanes, like friendly neighbours met for a gossip. Some, of a less sociable nature, had set themselves right in the heart of the fields.' Closer inspection, however, reveals the tell-tale village earthworks (best seen between Bourton and Easton), and the empty crofts of vanished buildings at Coate and around Bishop's Cannings church. Tax and population returns show that, rather than friendly neighbours, the houses are really just the survivors of once quite populous and wealthy villages. In 1332 Bishop's Cannings (with its satellites) exceeded the combined wealth of the three most prosperous settlements elsewhere in the Vale (Pewsey and the two Lavingtons), and almost equalled their combined population in 1377.

Shrinkage, movement, or complete desertion can be shown to have occurred in about 30 (or one-half) of the settlements in Pewsey Vale, and is fairly evenly distributed. In some places, as we have seen, earthworks survive to testify to the position of former village houses; good examples are visible in the fields between the two churches at

East Wick, seen from the escarpment near Martinsell. Former village earthworks survive in the field fringed by trees, in the centre of this photograph.

Alton, or south of West Lavington, or looking down towards East Wick from the Martinsell car park. Elsewhere the earthworks may not be very obvious, but early maps and the shape of the present settlement point to contraction. This is well seen at Conock and Fyfield. Both lie within the parishes of more successful neighbours (Chirton and Milton Lilbourne respectively), and both have linear plans which have atrophied while their neighbours (also with linear plans) have flourished. At North Newnton it was the mother settlement which was virtually abandoned (on account of flooding), and its daughter, Hilcott, which prospered. At Wilsford a kind of schizophrenia induced by two manor houses, at opposite ends of the street, pulled the village apart and left an open area (as at Etchilhampton) in between.

Movement in a village sometimes occurred in piecemeal fashion, sometimes for a specific reason, and sometimes at the whim of a landowner. At Huish and two of the Manningfords (Abbots and Bruce) their churches mark the positions of the small medieval villages; their successors lie, for the most part, further north. At Huish in the 19th century there was a third area of settlement, now abandoned, on the hill beside Gopher Wood. At Patney too the church is the medieval benchmark, but the more recent settlement was pulled along the road towards the (now defunct) railway station. The odd street plan of

Stanton St Bernard is the result of successive desertions, movements and rebuildings. In two instances certainly (and perhaps also at Conock) the present village plans are the result of movement imposed by a landowner. At Rushall in the later 18th century Edward Poore moved part of the village away from the house he had built for himself next to the church, and resited it along the present main road. His house is now only a large mound, and the church stands by itself, but the thatched estate cottages remain where he transplanted them. At Wilcot (see Walk 1) a more ambitious scheme was adopted by the Wroughton or Montagu family at the same period to remove the village of East Stowell (inconveniently close to their seat, Stowell Lodge) and rehouse its inhabitants in estate cottages built around a triangular green next to the Pewsey–Devizes road.

The most extreme form of shrinkage is total desertion, but this is rare in Pewsey Vale. On the valley floor we may cite three examples: Milcot lay beside the river north of Milton Lilbourne. There is a trout farm there now, and the old name has been corrupted to Milkhouse Water; the settlement seems to have transferred to nearby New Mill in the 18th century. Isterton is the name given on early maps and surveys to a group of closes and small fields due east of Marden. Village earthworks survive in the area, so Isterton ('the eastern farm') is likely to have been the name of a small, now deserted, settlement. Less than a kilometre downstream from here is Puckshipton House, the successor of a house which replaced a small medieval settlement on the site. The name means 'goblin's cattle-shed'. On the less hospitable chalk hillsides desertion is more understandable, especially after population totals tumbled and the economic climate changed after the Black Death epidemic of 1348-9. Gore lay on Salisbury Plain above West Lavington; it had a medieval chapel dedicated to St John and stood at an important cross roads of downland tracks. There is a farmhouse and a barn there now, with a rather unpleasant pond beside the main A360 road. Far more isolated is Shaw, which lay next to Wansdyke high on the downs above Alton. A large area of village earthworks survives from a settlement which seems to have been deserted in about 1400 – only three taxpayers lived there in 1377, and no-one was recorded in 1428.

Taxation and census records chronicle the losers, such as Shaw, but they also highlight the winners. Several communities, for instance, which lay along the line of the Kennet and Avon Canal showed an upturn in fortunes during the early-19th century. The population of Wootton Rivers rose by 50% from 313 in 1801 to 470 in 1841. Next door, at Milton Lilbourne, a dramatic rise in population between 1377 and 1676 may be linked to the northward expansion of the village from its medieval core around the church, along its street to the cross roads with the Pewsey–Burbage road. Burbage too (although the data are incomplete) grew considerably from a collection of medieval forest-edge hamlets to a community which by the 19th century numbered 1,500 inhabitants; its rise may be connected with greater use of its street as a main thoroughfare, changes in the management of Savernake Forest, and the arrival of the canal.

The greatest winners, however, were the settlements which were already larger than average, and whose ancestry lay in the probable Saxon estate centres which were identified in the previous chapter.

Wootton Rivers lock. The canal, which passes close to the centre of the village, brought a new impetus to this isolated community. For boatmen travelling east this was the first lock they would have encountered since Devizes.

Informal cottage development at Urchfont Bottom used the chalkface as a back wall, and in places the occupants excavated into the chalk , presumably to extend their accommodation. The cottages have gone, but the marks in the chalk remain.

Potterne, with its complex plan, noble church, and long involvement with the bishops of Salisbury, seems to have increased its population almost threefold between 1377 and 1676. If reliable, the 1676 figure of 1,000 adults would make it larger than anywhere else in the Vale at the time except Urchfont – although the total doubtless included two small clayland villages, Marston and Worton, which were its satellites. Like Potterne, Urchfont seems to have grown substantially between the 14th and 17th centuries. Informal and squatter development associated with this expansion spread over common land west of the village, at Uphill and in Urchfont Bottom (see Walk 6); this has served to complicate what may earlier have been a simple linear plan running from the church and pond along the High Street to the present B3098. A third estate centre, Upavon, seems to have experienced two periods of growth. In the early middle ages an attempt was made to convert it from a large and wealthy rural manor into a small town. As a result its plan retains an urban feel, with a small (currently sadly disfigured) market square, which its later modest tax and population figures do not really justify. However, after the establishment in the parish of the Central Flying School in 1912 its population rose rapidly, almost quadrupling between 1911 and 1971.

Even so, no-one today thinks of Upavon as a town. But there are two places in the Vale, Pewsey and Market Lavington, which hover between village and small town status. Pewsey's share of the wealth and inhabitants of its Vale (less the exclusions noted above) has risen from just over 7% in 1332 to about 9% in 1377 and 1576, nearly 11% in 1676 and 1811, 16% in 1911, and over 20% and rising since 1981. The arrival of the railway in 1862, and the survival of its station to the present day, offering direct services to London, have been important factors in its success. Its pre-eminence after World War II was not in doubt, and Timperley in his book about the Vale in 1954 wryly noted the presence of

Pewsey is one of the estates listed in King Alfred's will. To celebrate George V's coronation in 1911 this statue of Alfred was erected two years later. River Street, with the former Phoenix Inn, runs away behind him and the thatched Phoenix Row of 1823, the former workhouse, is on the right. Alfred is glaring at the fire station.

Traditional platform sign, Pewsey railway station

the only cinema, alongside shops, banks, inns, garages, bus office and fire station, as a sure sign of Pewsey's capital status.

Pewsey's medieval success, however, is obscure. Its topography suggests that the original nucleus was an area around the church and River Street, which was formed into an island by two branches of the river (Pewsey means 'Pefe's island'). This, together with many satellite hamlets, constituted the large rural estate familiar to King Alfred, whose statue, since 1913, has been dodging the main-road traffic passing through it. It seems never to have acquired a market charter, but two planned medieval extensions, north along North Street and east along High Street, enlarged the original settlement (the once wider High Street, in particular, offering scope for trade and marketing), and accommodated a total population which by 1676 probably exceeded 1,000.

Market Lavington's bid for urban status is better documented, and fits a pattern seen elsewhere in Wiltshire. The early medieval village probably extended south-eastwards from its Saxon predecessor on the high land around the church to Broad Well (see Walk 5), so that, with White Street (part of an important early routeway), a triangular green was formed. But in 1254 one of its manorial owners obtained a charter to hold a Wednesday market in the village (which hitherto had been

Broad Well, Market Lavington, probably the village focus before it became a small town

known as East Lavington); it was presumably he who set about making a planned extension, with a market place, to the north-east of the existing village. The market place lost its character between 1958 and 1961 when the houses surrounding it were demolished, and now has the appearance of a car park for the old people's bungalows which were built on their site. But the High Street still retains behind the rectangular gardens on its southern side the hallmark of medieval planning, a straight rear boundary and footpath, which turn inwards at the limits of the urban extension. Like several other Wiltshire places similarly promoted in the 13th century (Sherston, Lacock and Amesbury, for instance) Market Lavington never became an important town (Devizes is too close), but the range of shops and services which it still provides marks it out, like Pewsey, as something special within the landscape of villages dotted along the Vale.

5
ANATOMY OF A
VILLAGE

OUR EXPLORATION OF villages – shape and position, rise and fall – has so far had little to tell us about the individual units which have come together to create what we recognise as a village. But now the time has arrived to begin taking the village apart, and to see what its constituent parts are made of. With this in mind I visited and have revisited Woodborough, which I had chosen more or less at random.

At the point where the village street turns and broadens, to reveal a long view of blue-green hills behind grazing friesians, stands the flint Victorian church surrounded by its congregation of tombstones within a far older churchyard. Across the lane, secure behind high walls and foliage, is a large, rendered, 19th-century former rectory, and beyond the churchyard hides a neat Queen Anne farmhouse of blue and red bricks on a stone plinth. Looking back down the street I saw an assortment of village houses and cottages, the older ones timber-framed and thatched, others of brick and tile, some rendered, a pair of estate houses, and various modern dwellings. The lane peters out beyond the church, and here are a Wesleyan chapel and a school, both now converted to other uses. Nearby, across the field, is the brick and thatch manor house (a former farmhouse), and where the turnpike road crosses the parish, beyond the millstream, a cluster of houses is to be seen, near the site of a former pub, with the lane to the smithy beyond. A cursory glance around most villages in the Vale would reveal much the same picture, and so Woodborough may serve to set the agenda for this chapter about village buildings: first the church; then the gradation of domestic buildings, from manor house to roadside cottage; then the communal buildings, including the chapel, pub and school.

The church must come first, not only because in most villages (unlike Woodborough) it is the oldest building – usually a survivor from the middle ages – and the one most likely to be accessible to visitors, but also because the medieval church fulfilled many roles beyond its purely religious function. It was generally the most substantial building in the village, built of the local stone (flint, sarsen or greensand) rather than timber and mud, and it served as the community centre, for meetings, entertainment and education, safe deposit, even perhaps defence.
To a large extent the building itself mirrors the ups and downs of the community and the attitudes of its aristocrats; so it becomes for us a kind of historical document, a barometer of local fortunes.

We think of the parish church, but of the 38 medieval places of worship recorded within our area, no fewer than 28 may be assumed (on either architectural or documentary evidence) to have been established before about 1200, at a time when the system of parish organisation, based on the payment of tithes, was still evolving into its eventual shape. Some churches in the larger places such as hundredal centres probably began as minsters, the headquarters for a group of priests whose job it was to evangelize the surrounding countryside. We may guess (for there is only circumstantial evidence) that Potterne, Pewsey, Upavon,

Woodborough's Victorian church

and perhaps Bishop's Cannings and Urchfont may have been of this type. But most of our 38 started out as the private churches provided by landowners for the inhabitants of a tithing or estate. Wilcot church, for example, belonged to Edward of Salisbury and was new in 1086, according to Domesday Book. Allington, which never became a parish church, and has now disappeared, belonged to the manorial lord before 1100, because in that year he gave it away as part of his endowment of an abbey. When the parish boundaries were eventually settled Allington was regarded as a tithing of All Cannings, and its church became a chapelry of All Cannings parish church. At Chirton a church presumably existed in Saxon times (Chirton means 'farm by the church', and is so-called in Domesday Book); it must have belonged to the landowning family, because they granted the profits from it, and then the church itself, to Llanthony Secunda Priory at Gloucester during the 12th century.

Such privately owned churches are described as proprietary, and most of them by 1200 were, or were soon to become, parish churches. But, like Allington, several never achieved parochial status – Alton Priors, Draycot Fitzpayne, Eastcott (now part of Easterton), Etchilhampton, Gore, Manningford Bohun, Shaw and Stert all had medieval chapels-of-ease, dependent on parish churches in nearby villages. Occasionally we seem to see the process of parish formation at work. Upavon had a church at the time of Domesday Book, 1086, which may originally have been a minster, but was at that date controlled by a Norman abbey, St Wandrille de Fontenelle. St Wandrille, then or soon afterwards, also had claims over churches or chapels at Rushall, Charlton, Wilsford and Manningford Bohun, together forming a discrete (if somewhat irregular) block of land which may once have been the preaching territory of the former minster priests. Rushall was receiving its own tithes by 1142, so it was becoming a parish church, but it did not have its own graveyard (another mark of parish status) until 1395. We do not know when Charlton became a parish, although the earliest references to it are as a chapel. Wilsford also became a parish, but Manningford Bohun did not; it was joined to Wilsford as a dependent chapel, even though the two places were some four kilometres apart and separated by the parish of North Newnton. This curious arrangement, whereby a parish church had control over a detached or distant chapelry, occurred usually when both

Alton Priors church stands a short stroll away, past the earthworks of its shrunken village, from its neighbour Alton Barnes. But it was dependent on the church at Overton in the Kennet valley beyond the downs. The position of the church is interesting. It sits on a slight mound, beneath which massive sarsens have been discovered, close to a 'holy' well, and the yew tree in the churchyard is reputed to be 1,700 years old. If true, this means that the church was sited to be next to the tree – a church in a treeyard, rather than a tree in a churchyard.

communities were in the same ownership. For the same reason residents of Alton Priors were served only by a chaplain under the control of the parish church of Overton, more than six kilometres across the downs, even though there was a church with a rector and full parish rights virtually on their doorsteps, at Alton Barnes.

　　If a village grew and prospered during the middle ages, or if ownership of the manor passed to a wealthy individual – a baron or great estate owner – or a foundation such as an abbey, it was quite likely that the church would be rebuilt and enlarged, perhaps several times. This did not always happen, of course. The small communities at Alton Barnes and Manningford Bruce have retained their buildings – the former Saxon, the latter Norman – with much of the character of an original proprietary or estate church. At Patney and Stert the

The exquisite church at Alton Barnes. The nave is one of the most complete Saxon buildings in England, and is complemented by a miniature brick chancel, dated 1748.

little buildings there now are Victorian, although both are said to be faithful copies of their medieval predecessors. Some communities, as we have seen, disappeared entirely during the middle ages, and then their place of worship went with them. Shaw, high on the downs, had a chapel slightly larger than the nave of Alton Barnes, its parish church. It was remembered by tradition, though by no documents, and in 1929 its reputed site was excavated to reveal its foundations; it appeared that windows from Shaw had been taken at some date for re-use at Alton Barnes. Gore, too, had a medieval chapel, but this was recorded in documents, and is known to have stood unused in about 1550; the foundations of its simple nave and chancel were uncovered in 1877. Huish nearly suffered the same fate. Its 13th-century proprietary church, which had full parochial status, was probably neglected in the 16th century, refurbished around 1609, in disrepair again by 1672, and in need of complete rebuilding soon after 1751. The present church, shorter than its medieval predecessor, dates from 1785 and 1879, but archaeological work undertaken in 1965-6 exposed part of an aisle chapel and other details of the original building.

Most of the Vale's churches, however, have enjoyed a happier history, and their surviving fabric bears witness to successive improvements and enlargements. Good examples of multi-period medieval churches are Market Lavington, Milton Lilbourne, Pewsey and West Lavington (see Walk 5) – all communities which achieved better than average growth, and so could afford to spend money on their churches. But the most influential improvers were the monasteries into whose hands the majority of the Vale's churches had fallen by the 14th century. Control of a church usually passed to a religious house in the form of a bequest by its lay proprietor, the successor of the landowner who had built it. The monastery (or it might be a cathedral or, later, an educational or charitable foundation) could become the rector, thereby entitled to receive the tithes as income, and employing a vicar to take charge of the spiritual duties (this was known as appropriation); or it might use the tithes to subsidize one of its officials, who was then responsible for employing the vicar (this arrangement involved setting up a prebend); or it might merely retain control of the choice of who was to be appointed rector, and therefore to receive the tithes (this control was the advowson).

Each of these arrangements existed in the Vale, and monastic involvement in these ways has affected the architecture of its churches. Chirton, for example, was appropriated by the canons of Llanthony Secunda Priory in 1167, who almost immediately, and greatly to their credit, rebuilt it; the late-Norman arcades and the fine timber roof are among the features which survive as evidence of how wisely they spent their money. At exactly the same period Wilcot church, appropriated by Bradenstoke Priory (near Lyneham) in 1182, was rebuilt, although only the chancel arch survives of this work. A little later, in 1227, Wilsford church was appropriated by St Nicholas's Hospital, Salisbury, and a new chancel was the result. Most impressive of all, at Urchfont in 1302 almost the entire church was rebuilt in lavish style at the expense of St Mary's Nunnery, Winchester (who owned the advowson), following an order by the archdeacon to rebuild the chancel (see Walk 6). The new work included transepts and a vaulted chancel roof – a great rarity in a village church.

Most of the monasteries which owned or controlled Pewsey Vale churches lay in Wiltshire or a neighbouring county. Ivychurch Priory

The vaulted chancel of Urchfont church

(near Salisbury) took over from St Wandrille the churches of Charlton, Rushall and Upavon; Shaftesbury Abbey had Beechingstoke; Cirencester Abbey had Milton Lilbourne and Pewsey, although the latter passed to Hyde Abbey, Winchester, along with Manningford Abbots; St Swithun's, Winchester, had Patney. Nunneries required male priests to officiate at their services, and these could be supported by prebends. North Newnton and Stanton St Bernard helped to finance prebendaries in Wilton Abbey, and part of the tithes of All Cannings endowed a prebend at St Mary's Nunnery, Winchester. Cathedrals, too, needed prebends to support their officials, and Burbage, Potterne and West Lavington contributed to Salisbury Cathedral prebends. Links of this kind were all-important in determining whether a church would be kept in repair, or allowed to deteriorate. The attitude of the manorial lord, too, especially if

Late- medieval lierne vault beneath Bishop's Cannings majestic tower and spire

he was also a churchman, might affect the fabric. Potterne and Bishop's Cannings were manors of the bishops of Salisbury; consequently they both have large, prestigious churches with more than a whiff of Salisbury Cathedral about their architecture.

There was another way in which landowners and other influential members of the local community enhanced their churches. Medieval religious life set great store by the efficacy of prayers for the dead as a means of ensuring the soul's salvation. Behind most bequests of churches to monasteries was a condition, implicit or explicit, that the monks would pray for the souls of the departed benefactor and his family. Another way of achieving this protection was to leave money as an endowment to pay for a priest, and for a special chapel within the parish church, known as a chantry, where he could perform regular masses for the departed. West Lavington had two such chantry chapels, provided by the Beckett and Dauntsey families, and both continued as family chapels and mausolea after the reformation; the Dauntsey Chapel is entered by a 16th-century arch, which is emblazoned with a pattern of the letter D (see Walk 5). At Charlton the north chapel was provided by William Chaucey in 1523 as the place of burial for himself and his wife, and as a chantry for a priest to pray for their souls for ten years. The architecture incorporates his coat of arms, and there is a memorial brass recording the gift 'Off yo'r charite pray for the soul of Will'm Chaucey gentylma' & Marion his wyfe which Will'm edefied thys Chapel...' Other chantry chapels are to be found at All Cannings, Burbage, Market Lavington, Urchfont and elsewhere. At Wilsford a 14th-century chapel had by the 18th century been fitted up as a schoolroom; it was later used as a bakery and was demolished about sixty years ago.

The private benefactions of the wealthy and the communal zeal of the parishioners combined to adorn many churches during the two centuries before the reformation. In particular the 15th century saw a vogue for building towers, in the Vale as elsewhere, and these survive in many villages, even when, as at Charlton, Stanton St Bernard, and Rushall, much of the rest of the church was rebuilt. At Charlton the rebuilding obscured the tower clock which now, apparently, can only be seen from the top of the escarpment to the south. Good examples of 15th-century towers may also be seen at All Cannings, Marden, Pewsey

Potterne church from the south-west

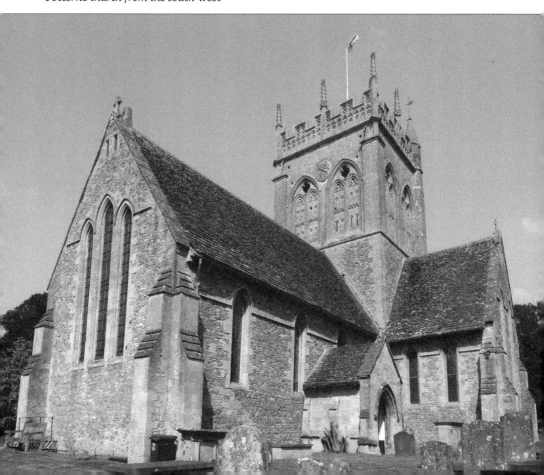

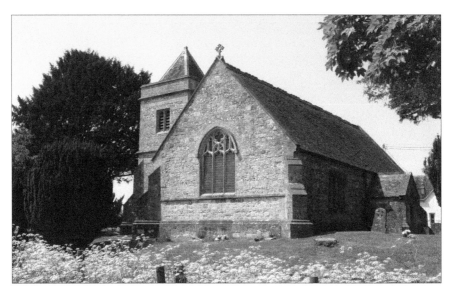

Easton Royal's Elizabethan church, built in 1591

and Urchfont, whilst at Potterne the large squat tower of the 13th-century church was crowned with elegant pinnacles and battlements in 15th-century style.

The reformation brought to an end almost all innovative church building, and for nearly three centuries from about 1540 most work on the fabric of churches took the form of patching and renovation. The one major exception in the Vale was at Easton Royal, which has an unusual history. Apart from very small cells belonging to French abbeys at Upavon and Charlton the only monastic house in our area was Easton Priory. This had been established in 1245 as a house of the Trinitarian order (one of only ten in England), and part of its duties was to cater for travellers. Easton already had a parish church, but this was demolished in 1369, and the Trinitarians' church was thereafter used also by the parish. Despite a serious fire in 1493 the church still served priory and parish until 1536, when the former was dissolved, and continued in an ever more ruinous state as the parish church until 1590. The owners of Easton, the Seymour family, then built the parish a new church on its original site and created a large house where the priory had been. The house has long gone, although earthworks, probably of its gardens, are still visible; the church of 1591 survives, but the present fabric is largely from a Victorian restoration in 1852-3.

If church building virtually ended at the reformation, the adornment of interiors, with woodwork, monuments and sculpture, continued. There are, it is true, notable earlier fittings, such as the impressive Saxon font with a Latin inscription at Potterne, interesting Norman fonts at Chirton, Upavon and elsewhere, and a 14th-century image of Gabriel at Etchilhampton (see Walk 2); but it is the extravagant and sometimes boastful monuments of later centuries, and the Jacobean woodwork, which more often catch the eye. William Button's arrival at heaven's gates is illustrated on his tomb

The pearly gates open to welcome William Button from his coffin, Alton Priors church

The elaborate memorial to Henry Danvers (died 1654), a descendant of the Dauntsey family, in their former chantry chapel in West Lavington church

Monuments to New College men, including Hare and Crowe, at Alton Barnes

in Alton Priors church (he died in 1590); Henry Danvers, who died in 1654, stares disdainfully at visitors from beneath his curriculum vitae in West Lavington church; whilst William and Joan Ernle have recorded their belief in personal salvation on a monument of particularly high quality at All Cannings. Less grandiosely, a glance inside Alton Barnes church leaves no doubt that New College, Oxford, held the advowson; the walls are lined with discreet monuments to New College men (including Augustus Hare) who served the cure. The Alton churches also retain attractive old wooden pews and, at Alton Barnes, a small gallery, as well as modern engraved glass by Laurence Whistler, who lived nearby; other good woodwork may be seen at Marden and Milton Lilbourne, whilst at Bishop's Cannings there is a most unusual piece of furniture, a penitential seat for contemplation, inscribed with a gigantic hand and doom-laden sobering mottoes in Latin.

    Religious enthusiasm during the 19th century took many forms. Nonconformist chapels we shall encounter shortly, but within the established church Victorian confidence and money transformed the parish churches, and people's attitudes towards them. Hardly a church in the Vale was left untouched by the restorer. Some, such as Beechingstoke and Woodborough, were almost entirely rebuilt on their existing sites; others were rebuilt except for a medieval tower and a few

Manningford Bruce, a small Norman church, sensitively restored by J L Pearson in 1882

fragments, as at Burbage and Stanton St Bernard; occasionally, but not often, restoration was carried out with great sensitivity and attention to medieval detail – Manningford Bruce is a delightful example, and Pewsey is interesting because much of the beautification was the work of the rector, Canon Bouverie, and his family. Canon Bouverie also installed over his vestry a medieval roof taken from the refectory of Ivychurch Priory. But besides the work of restoration and rebuilding (often, it should be added, entirely necessary to prevent collapse), the Victorians also reorganised parishes, and new churches were built accordingly. Three schemes were implemented for dual-purpose buildings (church and school combined) in hitherto deprived villages, at Hilcott in 1851, Easterton in 1867-75, and Coate in 1876. Oare was provided with a striking brick church in 1858, and at Manningford Bohun a strange compromise was reached. The tithing had two centres of population, the older nucleus at Bohun itself, and a more recent ribbon hamlet at Bottlesford. To serve them both a church, with grotesque crazy-paving masonry, was built in an isolated position on Manningford Bohun Common, mid-way between the two settlements. It was closed in 1973 and is now a private house.

With these relatively few exceptions the churches of the Vale, and
of rural England generally, are medieval in origin beneath a Victorian
veneer. With domestic buildings, of course, the picture is very different.
Of the 6,000 or so houses in the Vale, only a few retain medieval work,
and the vast majority have been built during or since the Victorian
era. We noticed when discussing population that the 20th century saw
the larger communities of the Vale grow larger still, whilst the smaller
stagnated or even declined. Housebuilding, as one might expect, has
shown a similar trend. Potterne and Upavon, for example, both increased
their housing stock by more than 40% during a single decade, 1961-71,
and large new housing estates have been built in recent years at Burbage,
Pewsey, Urchfont and the Lavingtons. Many of the smaller villages have
also acquired modern houses and bungalows, by infilling vacant plots, or
by replacing old with new. We noticed this at All Cannings, and it is well
seen at Easton Royal, and indeed at Woodborough, our starting-point for
this chapter.

Besides its modern houses Woodborough village has nineteen
listed buildings (although four of these are monuments in the churchyard
and one is a bridge). One is the church, and two are granaries on staddle

Church Farm, Woodborough, an 18th-century brick farmhouse, listed grade II

stones; eight more are houses and cottages which began life as timber-framed buildings under thatched roofs, although four have been refaced in brick. Brick has also been used to infill the panels of timber framing, although Church Farm Cottage retains some of its earlier wattle and daub infilling, and malmstone (a form of greensand rock) was used at One Yew and High Bank. By 1700 timber-framing was becoming obsolete, and brick started to be the dominant building material. Church Farmhouse, of about this

Timber cruck of a vanished cottage preserved in the wall of its neighbour Urchfont

period, uses blue and red bricks on a stone plinth under a tiled roof, and another contemporary farmhouse, now known as the Manor House, is also of brick, but with a thatched roof. The former rectory, of the early 19th century, is rendered, and its roof has slates – a commodity which became quite widespread in the Vale after the opening of the canal in 1810.

Woodborough's vernacular architecture is fairly typical of the area. It reflects the dearth of good local building materials. The nearest source of good limestone was in the Corsham and Box area of north-west Wiltshire, good timber was not plentiful, and the local rocks all presented the builder with problems. Sarsen from the Marlborough Downs was too hard to work into shape, greensand boulders tended to be broken up by frost (although a greensand plinth was often used as a kind of damp proofing), chalk was generally too soft, and flint came in small irregular nodules. When bricks became readily available during the 18th century from local brickpits (and after 1810, via the canal, from further afield), they offered a more durable and versatile medium, and were extensively used to reface and rebuild existing houses made of poorer materials. Likewise clay tiles, and later slate, began to compete with thatch, the traditional roofing material.

The humbler cottages of the 17th century and earlier have for the most part disappeared. They may now be grassed mounds in vacant plots along the village street, or their sites have been re-used for brick buildings, or they have themselves been rebuilt in brick. At Townsend in Urchfont one cruck from a vanished late-medieval cottage has been exposed as the gable of its later neighbour; and at Urchfont Bottom, in the sides of the chalk cliff, can be seen socket-holes for the joists of cottages which once used the cliff as their rear wall (see Walk 6). But in general it has been the more prestigious houses, built of better materials, and with more money available for their upkeep, which have survived to the present day.

Any study of high-status houses in our area – manor houses, principal farmhouses, and rectories – must begin with Porch House at Potterne. (It should be stressed that neither Porch House, nor any of the houses mentioned here, are normally open to the public.) Porch House was probably built, in the later 15th century, as the headquarters for

Porch House, Potterne

the bishop of Salisbury's bailiff or manorial staff, and, despite a varied subsequent career, it survived long enough to be taken up by the painter, George Richmond, and sensitively restored in 1876. It comprises an open hall with original roof and fine transomed bay window to the street, flanked at either end by cross gables, from one of which projects a smaller third gable over the porch which gives the house its name. Stout timber-framing is complemented by elaborately carved bargeboards and embellishments which give the house an opulent appearance. Medieval domestic architecture of a more modest nature survives sporadically in the Vale. A cruck-built house in Coxhill Lane, Potterne, near Porch House, was carefully recorded during renovation in 1980; it had a hall open to the roof as the central bay of three, with a parlour to one side and service rooms to the other. There are medieval cruck-built houses also at Wilsford, and at Market Lavington the Old House in Parsonage Lane retains part of a 14th-century hall; its construction may be linked with Edington Priory's acquisition in 1368 of the manor which this house subsequently controlled.

The capital messuages which were the hub of manorial organisation, and which, with their numerous outbuildings, are frequently described in medieval documents, were usually replaced by manor houses on the same sites during the 17th century or later. Good examples of timber-framed manor houses are at Etchilhampton, Eastcott and Wootton Rivers. Etchilhampton Manor may in fact incorporate some of its medieval predecessor; and Fyfield Manor, between Milton Lilbourne and Pewsey, retains the roof of the 15th-century manor house, surrounded now by the splendid early brick house of the mid-16th century and later. When Upavon Manor was rebuilt at the end of the 16th century old materials – chalk rock known as clunch, ashlar blocks and flint – were re-used, probably from a 'mean farmhouse' which had been built soon after 1488. At Urchfont the manor changed hands in 1678, and the new owner, Sir William Pynsent, decided to demolish the principal house and build a new mansion of local brick on the site (the former Urchfont Manor College, since 2013 privately owned), into which he incorporated a Tudor fireplace, oak panelling and some structural timberwork from its predecessor.

Pynsent's project at Urchfont involved extensive landscaping, but it was well away from the village nucleus on the former Upper Green.

Milton Lilbourne Manor

Elsewhere the lesser dwellings of the village might suffer from the squire's grand design. Milton Lilbourne Manor (of about 1710-30) enjoys an uninterrupted vista eastwards, but the mounds of former buildings fronting the village street at this point suggest that the view was gained at the expense of their removal. A later, and more ambitious, relocation scheme was the building of Stowell Lodge (completed in 1813), which, as we have seen, involved creating a new village around Wilcot Green to rehouse the inhabitants of the razed hamlet of East Stowell (see Walk 1). At Conock, between Chirton and Urchfont, two substantial manor houses were built in about 1700, Conock Manor of ashlar limestone, and Conock Old Manor of brick. At much the same period a brick manor farm was built nearby, thus enabling Conock Manor to become a gentleman's residence rather than a working farm. Most of the village houses and cottages disappeared during the later 18th and early 19th centuries (although two examples of about 1720 remain, one timber-framed and thatch, one brick and slate), and a fine ornamental lodge and pair of estate cottages were built instead.

Oare House

Conock, Urchfont and Milton Lilbourne are just three examples from a distinguished company of manor houses built in the Vale during the two centuries from about 1680. Other good 18th-century houses are Wedhampton House, of 1701, though built on an earlier timber-framed core; Clyffe Hall, Market Lavington, of 1737 with later wings; and Oare House, of 1740, approached from the main road by an avenue of lime trees, and with distinguished additions of 1921-5 by Sir Clough Williams-Ellis. Early-19th century houses include Rainscombe, above Oare, in a marvellous setting; Marden Manor, aloof from its village; and Stowell Lodge. Blount's Court at Potterne, which now presides over a housing estate, and Lavington Manor (now Littleton Pannell Manor, and part of Dauntsey's School), are imposing essays in Victorian Gothic and Victorian Tudor respectively.

Beneath the ranks of the gentry came the clergy and the principal farmers. Like other domestic buildings parsonage houses built before about 1700 tend to be timber-framed, and at Chirton a surviving timber-framed house, Yew Tree Cottage, has been identified as the vicarage house mentioned in a terrier of 1609. A timber-framed rectory (now the Old Rectory) was built at Manningford Abbots in about 1636, but it was refaced in brick early in the 19th century. The grandest of the brick rectories, and one of the earliest, is that of Pewsey, nine bays long, which between 1946 and 1993 served as the local council offices; other notable former rectories are at Alton Barnes and Huish.

Because enclosure came late to the Vale of Pewsey, unlike the claylands further west, farmhouses and farm buildings tend to be found lining the village street, rather than set alone among their fields. Exceptions are the outlying farmsteads of medieval or earlier origin, which often bear the place-name element 'wick' (East Wick and West Wick farms in the shadow of Martinsell are good examples); and the single farms which are all that remain of medieval manors or tithing centres, such as Huish, Draycot Fitzpayne, Puckshipton and Fullaway. Linear settlements may have several farmhouses (or former farmhouses) dotted along the village street (as at Easton Royal, Marden and All Cannings, for example), blending in with substantial yeoman's houses and farmworker's cottages. Not uncommonly there is a Manor Farm and a Church Farm, which date, as at Conock, from the period when the

The Old House, West Lavington, a timber-framed four-bay house of about 1600

squire and rector considered it no longer seemly for their residences to
be part of a working farm. Brick predominates everywhere in the Vale,
often colourwashed under thatch, or using vitrified blue-black headers
as decoration; occasionally, especially on Ailesbury estate housing
around Savernake Forest, polychromatic brickwork is employed in
gaudy designs. But there is also plenty of surviving timber-framing, for
example at Easterton, Horton, Stert and Wootton Rivers, as well as good
individual examples, at All Cannings, Pewsey (The Ball), Woodborough
and elsewhere.

Space does not permit us to examine all the buildings found in
and around villages. Reluctantly we must overlook the development of
rural council housing since the 1920s, the occasional village poorhouses
and almshouses, and the watermills (and very rarely windmills) which
were an essential feature of the agricultural economy. We omit too the
ubiquitous former village police constable's house (instantly recognisable
from its 'dolls-house' profile and rectangular plaque between first-
floor windows); and that curious blend of functionalism and ugliness,
the village hall (of which Urchfont's, mentioned in Chapter 8, is an
interesting example). Nor can we spare a second glance at those large
institutional buildings which happen to fall within our area. They include
the classical Pewsey Union Workhouse of 1836, which became a district
hospital in 1948, and then a unit for mentally handicapped patients
until closure for redevlopment in 1995; the county lunatic asylum,
built in 1851 within what is now Roundway parish on the outskirts of
Devizes and, as Roundway Hospital, another casualty of government
policy during the 1990s; the nearby Le Marchant Barracks, former
headquarters of the former Wiltshire Regiment, which dates from 1878;
and the stark blocks of RAF Upavon, now administrative headquarters,
but from its establishment in 1912 until 1942 the home of the Central
Flying School. Instead we shall concentrate on three categories of
building commonly found in Pewsey Vale villages: chapels, pubs and
schools. Shops and shopping will receive a little attention in Chapter 6.

Chapel-building (by nonconformists, as opposed to the medieval
and later chapels-of-ease of the established church) rarely occurred
before it was sanctioned by the Act of Toleration in 1689. The discontent
which gave rise to it, however, had been present in barely concealed form
for several generations among puritan clergy and more radical religious

groups such as Quakers. Before toleration we hear of Quaker families at Bishop's Cannings and Market Lavington, as well as an indefatigable Quaker, William Moxon, at Marden; the rectors of Pewsey and Alton Barnes were leading puritans during the Commonwealth; and at Burbage meetings were being attended by 30-40 Anabaptists in 1669. A census taken in 1676 suggests that there were then altogether nearly one hundred nonconformist adults in our area.

Of the older denominations two congregations are noteworthy. The Quakers of Market Lavington were meeting at the house of their leader, Isaac Selfe, in 1690, and had begun meetings also at Urchfont, Easterton and West Lavington by 1707. In 1716 they opened a meeting house at the east end of Market Lavington High Street, which they occupied until 1799. By then only one Quaker was left and the building was sold; it still survives, most recently in use as a studio, and is one of the oldest nonconformist premises in Wiltshire. Also in 1716 a private house in Rushall was being used for worship by a congregation of General Baptists who, following an endowment in 1743, built a chapel in 1760. From 1821 to 1864 a doctrinal dispute smouldered over whether or not the minister was upholding the religious principles demanded in the founder's trust deed; an ugly scene occurred in 1849 when an argument in the chapel between the minister, Mr White, and a trustee, Mr Black, threatened to become violent and a policeman had to intervene. Despite this, the Baptists of Rushall continued to worship until the death of their minister in 1956; the chapel was finally closed in 1973, and has now been demolished and replaced by bungalows, although the minister's house survives.

The period from 1750 to 1900 witnessed spectacular growth by new and revitalised nonconformist groups, especially the various branches of Methodism, the Independents (later known as Congregationalists) and Baptists. Cottage meetings were held, and later chapels were built, in most villages in the Vale, even though some, like the Baptist mission room at Etchilhampton, was nothing more than an iron hut. Woodborough Wesleyan chapel is typical. It was built in 1820 at the instigation of Thomas and William Shipman. They were local men – Thomas was the village baker – and they had been holding Methodist services for at least two years previously in William's house. Many members of their congregation worked at Honeystreet wharf. The

Woodborough Wesleyan chapel, now a private house

chapel continued to function until 1969, but after closure in 1970 it was converted into a pleasant private house.

The most flourishing congregations were generally to be found in communities without their own parish church, such as Hilcott (which became a centre for Independents), Manningford Bohun (where the Strict Baptist chapel survives alongside the main road), Bottlesford and Oare. An early Methodist group was meeting at Eastcott by 1757 under the superintendence of the saintly David Saunders of Littleton Pannell; he was to achieve fame as 'the Shepherd of Salisbury Plain' idolised in a popular religious tract by Hannah More. And at Market Lavington, which was poorly served by the Church of England, in the guise of an allegedly violent curate, the Independent denomination flourished, taking over the former Quaker chapel in 1801.

Besides their building at Manningford Bohun, which they called 'Providence', the Strict Baptists opened chapels at Upavon ('the Cave of Adullam'), Pewsey, and Allington ('Bethel'). Allington chapel, which is still in use, was built in 1829 by a local farmer and village

Bethel Baptist chapel, Allington, interior, and monuments to its founding fathers

evangelist, Joseph Parry, and attracted the support of an Oxford don, Rev J.C. Philpott, who seceded from the Church of England in 1835. In its heyday its influence extended far beyond Allington, as Philpott's son made clear in describing a service at which his father preached 'Peasants trudge in from miles around, bringing their dinners with them, till, even the gallery being full, the chapel overflows into the little graveyard, and

the late-comers join in the hymns and listen to the long prayer and longer sermon through the wide open casements . . . The two-hour service over, there is much vigorous hand-shaking outside, with hearty greetings in broad Wessex.'

Authority in the 17th century and later viewed chapels in much the same light as alehouses – places of sedition frequented by troublemakers. At Pewsey in 1646, as we shall see, an attempt was made to close down illicit alehouses. From the 18th century licensing records enable us to gauge their numbers and distribution. In 1737-9, for instance, eighteen communities in our area had a single licensed inn or alehouse, Littleton Pannell, Pewsey and Upavon had two, Burbage three, Potterne six, and Bishop's Cannings and Market Lavington nine each. The Bishop's Cannings total is explained by the inclusion of Devizes Green, with its numerous inns, within the parish at that date. The striking difference between our two urban centres, Market Lavington (nine premises) and Pewsey (two), may be explained largely by the main road traffic of the day (which we shall discuss in Chapter 6), but there is also the contrast between an open society at Market Lavington, which tolerated religious nonconformity as well as alehouses, and the more regimented and firmly controlled community at Pewsey, which discouraged both.

Of the 40 or so establishments licensed in 1737-9 the majority were alehouses, the precursors of the modern pub, but a few would have been inns, supplying respectable accommodation, stabling and food for strangers, as well as serving local needs. The Antelope Inn at Upavon, first recorded in 1609, is a good example; the predecessor of the present Phoenix Inn at Pewsey, which perhaps dated back to the 16th century, the Green Dragon at Market Lavington, and the George and Dragon at Potterne are others. The George and Dragon, in fact, was shown by a detailed survey in 1981 to be a late-medieval cruck building, and it may have been built as an inn during the period 1450-1500 by the landowner, the bishop of Salisbury. There are more modest village alehouses in 17th-century buildings at Wootton Rivers (Royal Oak) and Easterton (Rose and Crown).

Lists compiled between 1822 and 1827 show that there were then 33 licensed premises in the Vale of Pewsey. By 1880 the total was 43 and by 1935 it had reached 48; it is much lower now. Many of the names

The Antelope Inn, Upavon, overseeing the former market place

listed in the 1820s are still familiar – the Crown at Bishop's Cannings, the
Seven Stars at Bottlesford, and the White Hart at Burbage are examples.
In some instances the premises have since been rebuilt or the name has
been changed. The Poore's Arms at Charlton replaced a building called the
Red Lion which was burnt in 1821; because the arms of the Poore family
were supported by a leopard, the pub became known as the Charlton Cat,
and as a restaurant and tearoom this is its present name. At Easton Royal
the Gammon of Bacon was rebuilt on a new site and changed its name
in about 1850 to the Bruce's Arms, although locally even now it is often
still referred to as 'the Gammon'. At Wilcot an 18th-century alehouse
known as the Swan was called the White Swan in 1848, but was replaced
in 1859 by a building on a new site, and this was christened the Golden
Swan. At All Cannings the Kings Arms is listed from 1822, but the present
building carries the date 1880. At Woodborough, however, the pub has
not survived. An alehouse is recorded in 1737, and was probably the Rose
and Crown, which in the 18th century hosted meetings of Swanborough
hundred. It stood on the corner of Smithy Lane, and eventually became a
temperance hotel before being closed in about 1920.

Traffic generated by the canal and railways led to the building of new pubs. Pewsey wharf was served by the French Horn, and the hamlet of New Mill had its New Inn (now closed); near Horton a pub was built next to the canal bridge, and was appropriately called the Bridge, just as at the boatbuilding hamlet of Honeystreet (although actually across the parish boundary in Stanton St Bernard) the Barge was built. When a new main road junction was created near North Newnton in about 1840 the Woodbridge Inn was built alongside it, and hotels were built near the railway stations at Woodborough and Littleton Pannell. The latter was known as the Railway Hotel, but later as the Chocolate Poodle – it had received its licence in 1900 by transfer from a closed inn nearby called the Black Dog.

During the 19th century Pewsey seems to have made up for lost drinking time. In 1822 only the Phoenix was licensed, but it was joined by the Royal Oak in 1825. A directory of 1880 lists in addition the Crown, French Horn, Greyhound, King's Arms and Plumbers' Arms. Some of these probably resulted from legislation in 1830 which permitted 'beerhouses' to be operated from private dwellings. Other examples of Victorian beerhouses which became village pubs are the Lamb at Urchfont and the Three Horse Shoes at Little Salisbury, near Milton Lilbourne.

The Vale has always been better supplied with pubs than with schools. There are at present twelve primary schools, with an average attendance of 120. The largest are at Bishop's Cannings, West Lavington and Pewsey, with 204, 179 and 175 pupils respectively, the smallest at Chirton, with 26. There are also two small comprehensive schools for pupils up to 16, at Market Lavington and Pewsey (built as secondary modern schools in 1962 and 1957 respectively), which have 703 and 326 children on their rolls, and two independent schools, Dauntsey's, at West Lavington, and St Francis at Pewsey. This total compares with 26 village schools listed in a directory of 1880.

Before 1800 educational opportunities for children in the Vale were very limited. An enquiry in 1783 found that, of 24 parishes which replied, only four offered any form of schooling, and the sole long-established school was at West Lavington. This was a small grammar school founded by William Dauntsey in 1542, and held in one of the eight almshouses which still stand (although rebuilt in 1831) near the church. By the later 19th century it provided no more than elementary education, and after 1887 reorganisation of the charity took place. As a result the Dauntsey Agricultural School was built and opened in 1895 (the forerunner of Dauntsey's School), and a new elementary school was provided for the village in 1898. Two other private schools are recorded in 1739 at Potterne, for 50 poor children, built in 1712; and at Market Lavington, for 36 children. Both were probably quite short-lived.

Enquiries conducted in 1808 and 1819 found that by then most parishes had some form of very rudimentary schooling, either conducted by a 'dame' in her cottage, or by the parson or churchwarden as a Sunday school. During the 1830s and 1840s purpose-built day schools were provided in many villages, often with financial help from a Church of England body, the National Society. Some schools of this period were still in use until recently – the parish school at All Cannings was replaced by a new building in 1999. When an inspector visited it in September 1858 he found, 'a good schoolroom, with round-headed windows, moderately good desks and worn brick floor... The building at the time of my visit was enveloped in the foliage of a vine, laden with fruit, which was trained over the walls.' A middle-aged master and his daughter were in charge of between 70 and 80 children. Several of these early schools were thatched, including Bishop's Cannings, Easton Royal and Rushall, and at Manningford Bruce an attractive thatched school of about 1841 survives, although no longer in use as a school. Some village schools were very small. At Marden a charming brick and tile building of 1844 retains its bellcote, although its school career ended in 1925. The 1858 inspector found 20 children being taught there by a mistress of very limited attainments for 6 shillings (£0.30) per week in a schoolroom 12 x 24 feet (4 x 8m), with desks around the wall and the atmosphere very close. But that was as nothing compared with Charlton in 1859, where 30-40 children and their mistress occupied a room 13 x 10 feet (4 x 3m) – smaller than a typical modern living room. By contrast Burbage at the time of the inspector's visit had just been provided with a new school, through the efforts of the vicar, Thomas Stanton, and with support from Lord Ailesbury. It was well-lit and ventilated, with a good supply of books and apparatus, a boarded floor and parallel desks. This building, the National School of 1856, lies in Eastcourt opposite the church, and was abandoned in 1989 in favour of a brand new primary school nearby.

Burbage National school, opened in 1856 and closed in 1989. It was supported by Lord Ailesbury, and his love of decorated brickwork is in evidence.

Another wave of school-building followed the 1870 Education Act, which made school provision compulsory. A new school was provided at Broad Street in 1872. It lay in Beechingstoke parish, but became known as Woodborough School, because it lay close to Woodborough Station. It served a cluster of nearby villages, including Woodborough, whose own school, which we discovered down a path when we explored the village, was closed in consequence. Similar rationalisation took place at Rushall, where, also in 1872, the existing school was demolished and a new one (still in use) was built on a different site for children from Charlton and part of North Newnton, as well as Rushall itself. The surviving school at Easton Royal (now, and perhaps a little grandiosely, rebranded as Easton Royal Academy) is of the same period, and like Rushall and Woodborough, was built as a National (or Church of England) School. At neighbouring Milton Lilbourne, however, a non-denominational school board was formed to build and manage the school, which opened in 1878 but is now closed. A few years later, in 1887, the National Schools at Pewsey were taken over by an elected school board. Despite the strength of nonconformity in certain areas of the Vale there seem to have been no British (or nonconformist) Schools at all. There was however at Coate a combined school and chapel, affiliated to the Plymouth Brethren, which was built in 1848; but its educational role dwindled after Coate National School started up in opposition in 1876.

Although modifications and additions were frequently made, very few new village schools were built after 1880, the principal exceptions being Bishop's Cannings in 1907 and Oare in 1914. During the 1920s several of the smaller schools were closed, including Stert, Patney, Coate and Marden, and another spate of closures began in the 1960s; early casualties included Wilsford, Wilcot, Etchilhampton and Stanton St Bernard. In compensation new primary schools have been built, beginning with Upavon in 1957, Market Lavington in 1971, and more recently Burbage, Urchfont, Pewsey and All Cannings. One closed village school, Wootton Rivers, was taken over for use as a teachers' study centre.

There is something rather forlorn about a closed village school. It is a symbol that a community has lost part of its independence. The children now travel away to be taught about the world in a slightly different part of it. And their parents, for the most part, are not at home during the day; they work, shop, make friends, attend meetings and seek entertainments elsewhere, often many miles away. How all this travelling came about, and how it has diffused the local character of the Vale, must be our next concerns.

6

PASSENGERS AND OTHERS

OUR KNOWLEDGE AND enjoyment of Pewsey Vale is derived, unless we live there, from our ability to visit it. We drive around it, some of us pedal or walk along its lanes, we see it flash by from the window of a train, even chug by from the deck of a canal boat. Conversely, if we are fortunate enough to live in the Vale, we use the same means of travel to link us to the outside world. This chapter is about why and how people move about.

The change of attitude which has transformed a predominantly static and self-dependent rural society into a shrunken world of commuters and mass-produced retailers may be summed up in two quotations. The first, by a Victorian rector's daughter, recalls an old woman in Pewsey, reputedly a centenarian, probably during the 1840s. 'She told us she had been born at B– [Burbage, or perhaps Beechingstoke?], a village some five miles off; and with the exception of having been once or twice over the downs to E– [Everleigh?], a lonely village on Salisbury Plain, she had never left her husband's village since she had been married and settled there, about eighty years or so before! "She didn't hold by gadding."' The second is a remark made to a journalist in the 1930s by David Waite, a Bishop's Cannings shepherd. They were discussing ruddle, the red dye with which sheep were marked. 'But I an't zid no riddleman vur donkeys' years now. I gets all my riddle at the chemist's at 'Vizes now. T'ent used much nowadays.' The itinerant tradesman had gone, his obsolescent product now available only in the town.

Our concern, therefore, is with three types of movement: the long-distance traveller, such as the ruddleman, for whom tramping along

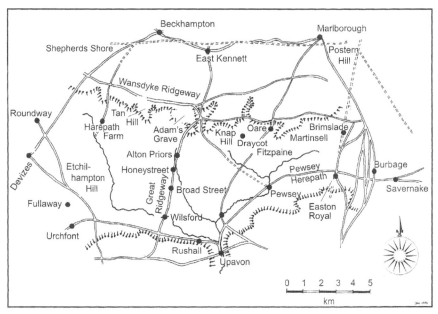

Early roads in the Vale of Pewsey

roads was a business; the trip into town, Marlborough, 'Vize [Devizes],
or further afield, for the occasional necessities of rural life; and the
village lanes and tracks, which those not given to gadding made use of to
take them from home to the fields, shop, pub and church. Before 1800
all such movements took place along varieties of road, and it will be
worthwhile to consider some of the characteristics of early roads still to
be seen in the landscape of Pewsey Vale.

Roads, like soils, are conditioned by the underlying geology, the
climate and human activity. Unless artificially maintained with stones
or tarmacadam, and kept in good repair, road surfaces deteriorate when
softened into mud by water and then disturbed by feet and wheels. In eras
of little or no organised maintenance the hardiest roads in our area have
been those crossing the chalk downland, particularly where they follow the
watersheds between drainage systems. Such roads, or ridgeways, benefit
from the porous nature of chalk and the absence of obstructing streams,
so as to be relatively indestructible and maintenance-free. Ridgeways
may be found running close to the edge of both northern and southern
escarpments overlooking the Vale of Pewsey.

But you cannot stay on high ground for ever. The road called
in the Vale the Lydeway, for example, a north-south downland route,

made good progress across Salisbury Plain, and was used until the 19th century as part of a main road from Salisbury to Devizes. But above Urchfont the chalk ran out and it had to descend to cross the greensand and gault of the Vale. Here the going was stickier, as the name of the nearby hamlet, Fullaway, 'the miry way', testifies. Even so, it clung to a watershed, that between the Salisbury and Bristol Avons, and as soon as possible it regained the chalk of Etchilhampton Hill to cross the downs north of Devizes. We have passed Fullaway, now we come to Roundway, 'the ridge way'.

The Vale posed precisely the same problem for the so-called Great Ridgeway, which has been traced running across the Chilterns, Berkshire and Marlborough Downs to Salisbury Plain and Dorset. Like Maria Hare at the beginning of Chapter 1, travellers along it from the north-east were greeted at Walker's Hill by the view across the Vale to Salisbury Plain. But far from being uplifted at the distant prospect, they would have envisaged the miles of possible quagmire in between. The probable line of the road as it traversed the Vale was by Alton Priors, Honeystreet, Broad Street, and a river-crossing near Wilsford. The names are significant: Honeystreet is 'the sticky metalled road', Broad Street 'the wide metalled road', Wilsford one of the few named fords in the Vale (see also Manningford below); and in addition there are references to the highway in neighbouring charters and field names.

The two modern main roads leading south from Marlborough (A346 towards Burbage and A345 towards Pewsey) are variations on the same theme. Both are probably Saxon or earlier. The A346 clings to the high ground of Savernake Forest to skirt the Vale through Burbage ('the fortified ridge' – it is the watershed between the Salisbury Avon and the Kennet); the A345 drops from the chalk at Oare, then the old road leaves its modern counterpart to follow the line of Hare Street (near Wilcot), cross the river at Manningford, and rejoin the high ground by climbing on to Bruce Down. The significant names in this case are the early names for Martinsell (*Mattelesora*) and Oare Hill (*Motenesora*), which flank the road's descent from the chalk. It has recently been suggested that *ora*, a Latin word which means 'steep bank', was borrowed by the Saxons to describe rounded hills which served as landmarks to guide travellers. Hence users of this route approaching from the south would struggle across Manningford and the valley floor with these twin peaks in view to guide them.

Roads on the valley floor might be improved by metalling or paving, as implied by Honeystreet and Broad Street. Often elsewhere 'street' refers to a Roman road, but only the dubious course of one Roman road has been identified crossing the Vale, and that has left no place-name or archaeological evidence. It is supposed to have run south from the Roman town of *Cunetio*, east of Marlborough, passed close to Brimslade, through Easton Royal (which may be aligned on it), and up on to Salisbury Plain. Minor lanes and tracks in the Vale were often raised on slight causeways. The north–south track which forms the parish boundary between Marden and Wilsford stands about a metre above the fields on either side, and east of Wilsford both the made-up road to Cuttenham and the bridleway across the fields to Charlton stand on slight causeways.

When roads encounter slopes two phenomena may be observed. On chalk hillsides a skein of parallel trackways may develop, as travellers pick the driest and least overgrown route up the rutted slope. The best local example is on Postern Hill south of Marlborough, but such trackways have sculpted both the Pewsey Vale escarpments, above

Parallel trackways ascending the northern escarpment to cross Wansdyke between Milk Hill and Tan Hill

Milton and Pewsey for example, between Milk Hill and Tan Hill, and above Oare. The effort involved and the damage caused to road surfaces on slopes when heavy loads were being transported is implicit in the name Draycot Fitzpayne, which lies at the foot of one such ascent. The first element is related to the modern word 'drag', and seems to denote a track up which sleds or wheelless carts could be pulled.

In the greensand area even the slightest slope tends to produce the phenomenon known as a sunken lane or holloway. Travelling feet loosen and damage the greensand road surface, which is then washed downhill, so that the road gradually cuts further and further down into the soft rock. The best-known examples close to the Vale are along the A360 Devizes–Salisbury road on either side of Potterne, but they occur also everywhere in the Lavington and Urchfont areas. The dramatic descent – of almost ravine proportions – down from The Three Graves, west of Urchfont, towards Crookwood, was probably in use in the Roman period since it served the area later known as Wickham Green, a name believed to indicate a Romano-British village in the area. On a more modest scale, the streets of many greensand villages have become holloways, so that cottage gardens bordering them stand one or two metres above the present road surface. A good example is the village street near Milton Lilbourne church, and we observed it too at All Cannings, in Chapter 4.

So far we have encountered long distance and local roads indiscriminately; indeed it is often difficult to decide who was using them. But sometimes their names suggest a particular function. Hare Street, for example, the road through Manningford and Oare, tells us by its name that it was a herepath (literally 'warpath'), or road used in the Saxon period by marching armies. Another herepath runs north-east from Horton across the downs towards Avebury, and is commemorated by Harepath Farm. And a third, known as the Pewsey Herepath, is now the B3087 Pewsey–Hungerford road; it is also remembered by a Harepath Farm, which lies next to the Burbage by-pass. The strategic importance of roads in the Saxon period is reflected in the fact that two battles took place (in 592 and 715) near Adam's Grave, which then had the pagan name of 'Woden's Barrow'. This was where the Great Ridgeway, also described as a herepath, had to cross the Wansdyke and then make a narrow descent between the frowning peaks of Walker's Hill and Knap

Hill. A military historian wrote in 1950: 'One feels that if a battle was not fought here one would have to invent one!'

A second function of long-distance routes, from prehistory until early this century, was for driving animals, and consequently many have acquired the name 'drove'. They were useful at local, regional and national levels. Locally they enabled shepherds and dairy-farmers to move animals from one pasture to another, and from farm to market. Nationally they formed part of a network of routes leading from upland Britain towards London and the Home Counties – drovers from South Wales crossed chalkland Wiltshire on their way to fattening pastures near the capital. At regional level droves served the annual fairs at Tan Hill, Upavon and Market Lavington, which we shall describe shortly. A venerable example is the Workway Drove, which leads from the Pewsey area through Wilcot up on to Knap Hill (the 'work' or earthwork of its name) where it joins the ridgeway along Wansdyke to Tan Hill.

Some indication of long-distance travel is provided also by the accommodation offered along the way. At Easton Royal the medieval priory had as one of its aims the succour of travellers, so we may assume that the village street, which is no longer a through road, was then part of an important north–south route. In 1646 a group of 28 parishioners petitioned to close illegal alehouses in Pewsey, arguing that, 'we haveing an inn in our parish which hath bin an inn time out of mind, which we know to be sifficient to entertayne all passengers and others that shall come through our parish uppon any occasion whatsoever'. Their petition is in fact a measure of how little passing trade Pewsey attracted. Devizes a generation earlier already had at least fourteen inns and numerous alehouses, and Market Lavington had at least seven inns and one alehouse. Travelling in general increased after the civil war, but Pewsey, as we have seen, still only had two licensed premises (compared with Market Lavington's nine) in 1737. A census of guest beds in inns and alehouses taken in 1686 suggests that most traffic in the Vale plied between Salisbury and Devizes. The road from Salisbury forked in the heart of the plain, and travellers could choose either the Lydeway down Redhorn Hill or the road through Market Lavington and Potterne. Of 61 guest beds recorded in the Vale 30 were at Market Lavington and 5 at Potterne, whilst 15 were close to the Lydeway, at Chirton, Urchfont, Etchilhampton and the hamlet of Lydeway itself. A further 6 were at

A remarkably deep greensand holloway leading to Crookwood below Urchfont

Burbage on the Salisbury to Marlborough road. No figure for Pewsey is recorded.

Occasionally we are told about specific journeys by individuals. At one end of the scale we know that in 1613 Anne, James I's queen, travelled back from Bath to London along the downland road from Lacock to Marlborough, which clips the northern edge of Bishop's Cannings parish. She paused, by prior arrangement, at Shepherd's Shore, where the entire parish was there to greet her, and under the supervision of its minister, George Ferebe, they presented a musical entertainment in rustic vein, which she apparently much enjoyed. Lower down the order in 1712 a manservant accompanying his lady on their way to Bath recorded his journey via Avebury, All Cannings, 'Vicese' Green and Potterne. All went well as far as Potterne, but then a hare crossed their path, and soon afterwards the servant fell from his horse with the luggage into a deep mire. More unfortunate still was Samuel Lawrence, whose battered body was found on the Lydeway near Chirton in 1795. It transpired that he had been on a journey from Lyndhurst to Hereford, carrying two bundles and a small box, and had stopped for lunch at an alehouse near Stonehenge. Here he was joined by another traveller, a stranger, and they left together. Samuel was not seen alive again, but later somebody recalled noticing the stranger – he was carrying two bundles and a small box – but by then he had disappeared.

To the inhabitants of the Vale the traveller, whether aristocrat, tradesman, drover, vagabond or thief, might be a source of irritation or excitement, and for some locals there was profit to be made from the passing trade. But for most people roads existed to serve their daily requirements and their occasional outings. Agricultural needs were served by a network of lanes and tracks which linked home to field and permitted stock and equipment to be moved from one part of the parish to another. The strip territories described in Chapter 3 often had the rural equivalent of a spine road, connecting all the grades of agricultural land. The Manningfords illustrate this well, and such a track survives too in almost all the escarpment tithings from Urchfont eastwards to Rushall. A second network of roads came into use on Sundays to enable everyone to attend church. Churchgoing was compulsory during the 16th and 17th centuries, and in a large, scattered parish such as Bishop's Cannings the combined mileage undertaken by a Sunday congregation must have run into hundreds. Consequently footpaths converge on many village churchyards, such as Urchfont, Bishop's Cannings and Milton Lilbourne. Coming to church in a coffin might pose special problems, for the bearers at least, and sometimes footpaths known as lychways or corpseways were maintained primarily for funeral processions. Such, it is said, was the path from Allington to the mother church at All Cannings.

Occasionally it was necessary to leave the Vale for business or pleasure in the town. This interaction between town and countryside may be recognised in the Roman period. A study has shown that distinctive grey or buff pottery, which was made in the 2nd century at sites near Broomsgrove (north of Milton Lilbourne), and perhaps at Martinsell and near Oare, as well as at the main production centre in Savernake Forest, was taken to market at the Roman town of *Cunetio* (Mildenhall). From there it became widely distributed throughout eastern Wiltshire, the Marlborough Downs, and further afield, especially to places close to the main Roman roads. A Saxon and medieval name for a road which led to a town was Portway, and so we find that fields in Urchfont abutting the Lydeway were still called Portway in the 19th century. Presumably the town in view was Wilton or Salisbury, over the hill and far away. Likewise the multiple trackways up Oare Hill, which led to Marlborough, were recorded as Portway as late as 1803.

As travel became easier in the 18th century (and especially after about 1850) trips to towns outside the Vale took place more often, as

A corner of Market Lavington's erstwhile market place, with its principal inn, the Green Dragon

we shall see; but in the middle ages more local trading satisfied most domestic and agricultural needs. Quite apart from itinerant chapmen, dealers and pedlars, local markets were established at Upavon in 1220 and Market Lavington in 1254; permission for a third, at Wilcot, was secured in 1221, but there is no record of it ever having taken place. Upavon's market continued through the medieval period and beyond, and, as we saw in Chapter 4, has given the village a modestly urban feel. Lavington's market continued until the 19th century, and in its later years was accompanied by many of the trades, such as malting, brewing, and small-scale engineering, which congregate in small market towns. Lively market scenes are glimpsed in the pages of an 18th-century magistrate's notebook. In 1748 William Hunt, esquire, convicted Hannah Beard of cursing and swearing six oaths in the market place, and sentenced her to ten days' hard labour when she refused to pay the fine; the previous year he had pacified an argument there between a Tilshead labourer and an Urchfont sack-carrier, which had come to a head when one had urinated in the other's hat.

Markets took place weekly throughout the year; fairs were annual events often associated with fixed agricultural requirements – dealing in sheep, cattle and horses, and hiring of labour. Besides the important town fairs such as St Denis's and the Candlemas fair at Devizes, and the Marlborough mop fair, more local fairs were held in August at Market Lavington, and in September or October in Upavon. An annual September fair at Rushall was permitted in 1285, but probably never took place. All these fairs pale into insignificance compared with Tan Hill Fair, one of several hill fairs held for centuries on the downlands of southern England. Its origins cannot be traced before 1499, when permission was granted for it to be held, 'in a place called Charlborough Down by Wansdyke on the feast and morrow of St Anne (26-7th July). 'Tan Hill' seems to be a corruption of St Anne's Hill (named after the feast), and not, as has been enthusiastically advocated, a relic of a Celtic fire festival (*tan* is a Celtic word for fire), out of which the fair has been imagined to have developed. Sheep, oxen and fineries, according to the 17th-century antiquary John Aubrey, were the commodities traded, but many other creatures, refreshments and entertainments were also on offer. The fair continued to be the highlight of Pewsey Vale's farming calendar until 1932, when it was held on its bleak hilltop above All

Cannings for the last time. Published descriptions of its latter years recall the early start, the flocks of jingling sheep-bells, the quarrelsome gypsies, the woman who sold cooked beans from a tub and, best of all, the occasion when the beer tent blew down.

Legislation made in the 16th century required parishes to take responsibility for maintaining their roads, and from the perspective of the villager who seldom ventured beyond his parish boundaries this was sensible and logical. Parish vestries appointed highway surveyors, who collected a rate and organised statute labour – four, later six, days in the year when, in theory, all able-bodied householders turned out to repair the roads. Failure to do so might result in a summons from the magistrate, an entire parish might be ordered to 'mend its ways', or a negligent surveyor might be reprimanded. At West Lavington in 1747 William Hunt the magistrate ordered one highway surveyor to pay the parish compensation of £2 because he had misappropriated twelve loads of flints intended for road maintenance.

Amateur roadmenders may have been acceptable in the 16th and 17th centuries, but by the 18th even remote rural areas, untroubled by

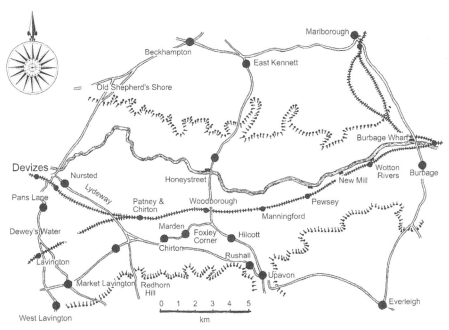

Turnpike roads, the canal and railways in the Vale of Pewsey

major roads, could not ignore the escalation of overland wheeled traffic and the gently quickening pace of national life. In the Vale of Pewsey the new order began in 1706-7.

The principle that travellers using troublesome (from a maintenance point of view) stretches of busy main roads should contribute to their upkeep was established in 1663, with the passing of the first turnpike act. In Wiltshire the justices applied this principle in 1706-7 by securing Parliamentary approval to turnpike several main roads, including part of the Lydeway, from Devizes to Etchilhampton Hill, and part of what now approximates to the A361, from Devizes to Old Shepherd's Shore above Bishop's Cannings. Travellers were charged tolls ranging from one shilling (5p) for a coach or waggon, to a penny (0.5p) for a horse, with cattle and sheep charged by the score.

Not for another 50 years or so were other main roads in and across the Vale turnpiked, and in this respect our roads reflect the national trend. The initial concern, with difficult stretches and the most heavily used roads of the kingdom, gave way by mid-century to a more general interest in providing a backbone for inland travel by improving the entire main road network, the precursor of the A and B roads designated during the 1930s. Between 1750 and 1762 the roads south from Devizes on to Salisbury Plain via West Lavington and Market Lavington were both turnpiked, as was the rest of the Lydeway up Redhorn Hill, and the present Marlborough–Burbage road through Savernake Forest, which then continued over the plain to Everleigh. At Foxley Corner, east of Urchfont, where the Lydeway begins its ascent on to the plain, it was crossed by other turnpikes, the present B3098 from Westbury (through Market Lavington and Urchfont), which then became the present A342 to Rushall and Upavon. Anyone who drives today from West Lavington along the scarpfoot to Upavon, may notice that the first two-thirds of the journey, through a succession of villages, is slow and difficult, whereas after the Chirton turning the going becomes faster and easier. An explanation, not too fanciful, is that the Westbury Turnpike Trust, beset by incompetence and recriminations, as we know it to have been, merely upgraded an existing jumble of lanes across the greensand, whereas the Andover and Devizes Trust wisely chose to ignore the tortuous lanes connecting Conock, Chirton, Marden, Wilsford and Charlton, and adopted instead a more elevated course across the lower slope of the

The lion monument at Stert commemorates James Long, who diverted the road in 1768

chalk, above the greensand which outcrops a few metres further north. Near the turning to Conock the two turnpikes joined, and here a tollgate is shown on a map of 1773; others were on the Lydeway at Nursteed (Devizes outskirts), on Redhorn Hill near the present vedette post, and at Dewey's Water between the Lavingtons and Potterne. One specific piece of improvement to the Lydeway undertaken in 1768 drove a new, less hilly road across the lower slopes of Etchilhampton Hill above Stert;

it is commemorated by the lion monument beside the road, which has become a landmark to thousands of travellers – indeed this stretch of road is known as Monument Hill.

Noticeable in this discussion of 18th-century roads is the absence of any turnpike in the Pewsey area. Pewsey in fact shares with Tisbury and Great Bedwyn the distinction of being the only communities approaching urban status in Wiltshire which were never visited by a turnpike road, and it is a measure of Pewsey's insignificance at the time as a trading centre. This was despite the efforts of the rector, Joseph Townsend, 'a strenuous advocate for the improvement of the highways', who in 1797 built a new bridge across the Avon between High Street and River Street, and like that better-known roadbuilder Thomas Telford was consequently dubbed 'the Colossus of Roads'.

Pewsey's isolation was dispelled in the 19th century by the arrival of the canal, but before considering that revolution we should mention one other turnpike venture, the Kennet and Amesbury Trust. In 1840, when it was established, road transport and the turnpike movement in general were bracing themselves for the disaster which railway competition was about to inflict. Very much against the tide, therefore, the local promoters of the Kennet and Amesbury Trust (one of the last in England) tried to improve road communications between Pewsey Vale and Salisbury, by opening up a route down the Avon valley to Amesbury. The stimulus may have been an earlier improvement further south, between Amesbury and Salisbury, and recognition that the canal, whilst satisfying the need for an east-west trading link, did nothing to connect the Vale with lucrative markets in the south. The trust therefore took control of the road across the Vale from East Kennett via Walker's Hill and Alton Barnes, Woodborough and Hilcott, to Upavon and south to Amesbury, with a feeder branch from Chirton and Marden. It enjoyed modest success until, like most turnpikes, it was wound up in the 1870s.

The tranquil canal, more than anything else, epitomises the Vale's gentle beauty. It meanders along its contour for nearly 25km without a single lock, from Devizes to Wootton Rivers, and since its restoration was completed in 1990 it has introduced the region's charm to many new explorers. The intention of its promoters in the 1780s was to link London and Bristol by a cheaper route for goods traffic than the overland alternative. They were not particularly concerned to benefit the inhabitants of the Vale; indeed until 1793 the proposed line would have taken the canal up the Kennet valley instead, via Marlborough and through a tunnel under Cherhill White Horse to Calne. The switch to its eventual route was determined by cost, time, and water supply.

Construction during the harsh economic climate of the Napoleonic wars was a protracted affair and, although work began in 1794, the Pewsey Vale section was not started until 1803, and only completed in 1809/10. On the last day of 1810 the Kennet and Avon Canal was open for vessels along its entire length, from the Kennet at Newbury to the Avon at Bath. The company built a wharf at Pewsey, and there were important privately owned wharves near Burbage (the depot for Marlborough) and at Honeystreet, where a boatbuilding and timber yard became an important source of local employment. Canalside pubs, with accommodation and stabling, were built alongside wharves at Pewsey (the French Horn), Honeystreet (the Barge) and New Mill (the New Inn, now closed); and on Burbage wharf still stands a large wooden crane, built in 1831.

Pewsey wharf

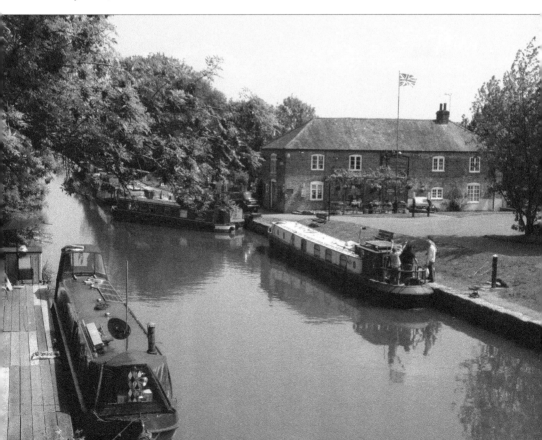

The Kennet and Avon canal near Horton

The new-fangled mode of transport was a source of fascination to local villagers. A Pewsey mother, contemplating emigration to Australia, sent her two little girls to watch the barges at the wharf, so as to give them some idea of the voyage that was in store for them. But the canal also brought tangible and immediate benefits, especially in offering a cheap supply of fuel from the Somerset coalfields. Stone for building and roadmending was carried, slates for roofs, salt, timber, metals and imported goods from around the world; very important, too, was the opportunity the canal offered to farmers of sending their produce to markets far afield. And besides the heavy barges there were fly-boats, which carried passengers and light goods rapidly along the Vale.

But the canal's prosperity was to last for no more than three decades. In 1841 the Great Western Railway between London and Bristol stemmed the revenue from long-distance traffic, and in response

the canal company proposed to make its own, competing railway along
its towpath. In 1846 it petitioned Parliament to build the London,
Newbury and Bath Direct Railway; and when this failed it sold the canal
to its competitor, the Great Western Railway, who presided over its
steadily dwindling traffic and deteriorating condition from 1852 until
its own demise in 1947. A report in 1909 showed that tonnage carried
on the canal had slipped from a peak of over 360,000 in the 1840s
to 210,000 in 1868, 120,000 in 1888, and 62,000 in 1905. The canal
limped on after the first world war, and its last regular commercial user
was probably the firm of Robbins, Lane and Pinniger, who owned the
wharf at Honeystreet, and who sued the Railway Executive in 1949 (and
won) over failure to maintain the canal. Accounts of later voyages are
surrounded by an aura of bravado, and throughout the 1950s the threat
of closure loomed. However, an association was formed to fight on the
canal's behalf, and as the recreational use of inland waterways became an
issue during the 1960s restoration was a feasible option. After 1965 the
Kennet and Avon Canal Trust conducted a restoration programme, which
culminated in the reopening of the canal by Her Majesty the Queen in
August 1990, 180 years after its original construction.

    Meanwhile the proposal to build a railway alongside the canal
was not abandoned. A line across Berkshire as far as Hungerford was
completed in 1847, and several proposals were floated to extend it along
Pewsey Vale to Devizes and beyond. By the time that it was opened, in
1862, there was already a line connecting Devizes with towns further west,
so its completion created a new through route across central Wiltshire.
The railway runs beside the canal east of Wootton Rivers, but then takes a
more southerly course, closer to Pewsey and past Beechingstoke. Stations
were opened near Pewsey and Woodborough, and by 1865 they were
served by four trains each way on week-days, and two on Sundays. Pewsey
residents woke up to the amazing realization that Devizes was now only
25 minutes away, Marlborough (which had its own branch) 35 minutes,
and they could be in London – yes, London – in a little over two hours. A
second facility was provided in 1900 by the construction of a railway which
left the Devizes line east of Stert, skirted the greensand edge north of the
Lavingtons, and connected with other lines at Westbury. In 1906 this was
incorporated into the Great Western Railway's direct main line to Exeter,
which is still in use, although the portion of line from Stert to Devizes was

closed in 1966. The Lavingtons were served by a station on the new line, and east of the railway junction a station, known as Patney and Chirton, was built in 1900. Between 1928 and 1932 additional halts were built at Wootton Rivers, Manningford, and Pans Lane on the outskirts of Devizes. Passengers using Wootton Rivers Halt had to buy their tickets from the village pub. Pewsey, which retains its original 1862 building, is the only station to remain open in the Vale.

Pewsey railway station

As their twin high-speed roars charge along the Vale the trains of today are one tangible reminder of the Victorian revolution in rural transport. Another is the way in which the railway affected the physical development of villages. At Stert, for example, the need for a railway cutting and bridge has twisted the village street – the twist and the bridge remain, although most of the cutting has been filled in. At Patney, as we saw, the village has extended northwards towards the now-defunct station – only an iron footbridge remains. And at Littleton Pannell the former Railway Hotel (subsequently the Chocolate Poodle) remains, though no longer an hotel, long after Lavington station has gone. But the railway's most significant achievement, continuing the process begun by the canal, was to open up the Vale, and to increase the distances and frequency with which country people travelled. A single example will suffice: in 1874 the licensee of the Blue Lion Inn at Collingbourne Ducis (10km south-east of Pewsey) advertised that he intended, 'running a break from Collingbourne to Pewsey Station, for the convenience of persons attending Devizes Market', every Thursday, leaving at 8.30 am to catch the 9.40 train, and returning home from Pewsey at 4.30 pm. Collingbourne did not lie within Devizes's catchment area – it was closer to both Andover and Marlborough – but the railway brought Devizes within reach.

With the outside world no longer cut off from the Vale, a thirst for travel developed. Many of the younger and stronger men of Pewsey are said to have walked to London and back in 1851 to visit the Great Exhibition, and a dozen years or so later Alfred Reynolds of Pewsey rode a penny-farthing bicycle to Hyde Park Corner and back within 24 hours. Towards the end of the 19th century the vogue for cycling led to the formation of the Pewsey Vale Cycle Club, and from its members in 1898 sprung the idea of the annual Pewsey Carnival. But it was in its link with the local towns – Devizes and Marlborough – that the Vale's change of attitude was most clearly seen. By mid-century a network of local carriers was developing, so that eventually most villages were served by a carrier's cart (sometimes two or more) trundling into town on market day. Devizes took the greater share of this traffic. In 1895 the line-up in the market place included carriers from as far east as Savernake, Manningford, Upavon and Wilcot. But from Pewsey eastwards most carriers went to Marlborough. Their journey took place on Saturday, market day, whereas Thursdays was natural for the Devizes carriers. The larger villages were served more frequently, and Edwin Potter ran a daily service into Devizes from the Lavingtons.

Accompanying the rise of the market town as service provider has been the decline of the village tradesman and shopkeeper. Where, for example, did you go when you wanted a new pair of shoes? In 1895 there were 16 boot and shoe makers, menders and dealers in Devizes, and another 16 in Marlborough; but there were also a further 44 scattered around the Vale – 6 in Pewsey, 4 each in Burbage and Wootton Rivers, 3 each in Urchfont and Market Lavington, and 1 or 2 in each of another 18 villages. Four decades later, in 1935, the shoe trade was based largely on mass-production with retail outlets. In Devizes there were 12 dealers, in Marlborough only 4, but in the Vale itself the 44 of 1895 had dwindled to 14, in just 10 villages. Telephone directories for 1999/2000 list 4 in Devizes, 3 in Marlborough, and none elsewhere. In 1895, therefore, if you wanted shoes you could probably buy them in your own village, or nearby; by 1935 you were much more likely to go into town; and now you have no choice.

And how, in 1935, would you have gone shopping to Devizes? On the train, perhaps, by bicycle maybe, or if you were well-to-do you might have a motor-car. But just as the canal foreshadowed the railway, so the carrier foreshadowed the motor-bus. Vehicles specifically designed to carry fare-paying passengers were rare in the Vale in the 19th century. Before the railway era stagecoaches had plied between Devizes and Salisbury via Market Lavington, and once the railway reached Hungerford a stagecoach service began from Devizes, via Pewsey and Burbage, to meet the trains. In 1848 it ran daily, under the slightly worrying name, 'The Surprise'. In 1855 and 1859 it ran from Market Lavington to Pewsey and Hungerford with a more reassuring title, 'The Hope'. Many years later, in 1895, the landlord of the Bruce's Arms at Easton Royal, Enos Price, described himself as proprietor and whip of the late Hope Coach.

But it was not until shortly before the first world war that the Hope's successor, the motor omnibus, made its appearance in the Vale,

Until the beginning of the 20th century travellers from Devizes and the western end of the Vale towards Salisbury would use the Lydeway and its continuation south across Salisbury Plain. The steep ascent up Redhorn Hill above Urchfont was followed by miles of rough downland. This major route was closed to the public by the army once the area became used for heavy artillery.

and then it was through the initiative of local carriers such as Cave of
Upavon. By 1915 he was running a motor-bus every Thursday between
Devizes and Salisbury via Upavon and Amesbury.

Services from Devizes to the Lavingtons and Marlborough also
operated, and after the war bus operation burgeoned at the expense of
the local carrier. Cave, and later Mortimer, served the Upavon area, with
buses from Pewsey and Woodborough to Salisbury, and Netheravon to
Devizes, timed to coincide with market days, church services and the
Saturday evening cinema. Wider-ranging and more frequent was the
network of services developed by Lavington and Devizes Motor Services
after its formation as a limited company in 1922. Its fleet of single-
deck saloon buses ran regularly between the Lavingtons and Devizes
(up to eleven times a day in 1926), with through running to Melksham,
Trowbridge, Chippenham and Bath. They also operated to Salisbury, and
provided a daily service to Urchfont and many of the smaller villages
between Pewsey and Devizes.

During the 1930s most of the local carriers disappeared from the
Vale – only Munday of Tilshead was still running into Devizes by 1939
– but the smaller bus companies were disappearing too. In 1948, when
most bus services were nationalised, the principal operators were Western
National and Bath Tramways Motors in the Devizes area, and Wilts and
Dorset around Pewsey and Marlborough. By now most villages along the
southern edge of the Vale had at least fifteen buses daily either to Devizes
or Marlborough, but the more sparsely populated northern edge could only
support one or two per week. An analysis of shopping patterns conducted
in 1949 showed that the whole Vale as far east as Pewsey and Upavon still
came within the catchment area of Devizes, whereas the villages from
Pewsey to Burbage looked north to Marlborough.

Of the roads themselves we have said nothing since the turnpikes.
Those trusts which staggered on beyond the arrival of the railways were
wound up during the 1870s, and responsibility for their roads passed to
short-lived highway boards (created after 1862 and abolished in 1888).
Thereafter the newly created county council became responsible for
main roads, and the rural district councils for minor roads. The Vale was
divided between Devizes R.D.C. (as far east as Alton Barnes and Marden),
and Pewsey R.D.C. (Alton Priors and Wilsford eastwards). This separation
of main (later classed A and B) roads and minor roads continued until

legislation of 1929 (implemented in full by 1933-4), which transferred the minor roads from the districts to the county council.

Road maintenance became a serious problem when military vehicles, horses and personnel invaded the plain from about 1900; the motor-car and heavy vehicles such as motor-buses made matters worse. By 1909 the county surveyor was advocating the use of a tar-sprayer on main roads, and in 1916 there were plans to spray about 350 miles of county roads in Wiltshire with tar, mostly derived from local gas works. Minor district roads were not tarred until much later. The first reference to tarred macadam in the Devizes R.D.C.'s minutes occurs in 1924, when it was proposed to treat the Alton, Stanton and Horton road, and the Chirton, Patney and All Cannings road, as well as others outside the Vale. In 1925 a small tar-spraying machine was bought for £145. Meanwhile traffic had been increasing, and in 1920 the county council held a census at Stibb Green, on the Marlborough–Burbage road, and on the bridge at Marden. The contrast is interesting. At Stibb Green, an important north–south road, nearly 40% of the traffic was motor-driven, and over 40% were cycles, with only 19% horse-drawn vehicles. At Marden, used mainly by local traffic, the proportion of cycles was slightly lower, but motor traffic accounted for only 23%, and horse-drawn vehicles almost 40%. Had you been sitting on Marden Bridge for an hour in September 1920 you would probably have seen three or four cyclists, one motor-car and one other motor vehicle (lorry, van or motor-cycle), as well as three one-horse carts or waggons, and one two-horse waggon. On average you would also have seen one horse (led or ridden) and three head of cattle.

Under the railway bridge in Pewsey in 1922, when another census was taken, passed 34 motor and 23 horse-drawn vehicles per hour. Where were they all going? Most no further than places in the Vale, one supposes, but increasing numbers were visiting the towns, and some were on their way to exotic destinations, like the bus listed in a 1927 directory which was said to pass through Upavon every Friday on its way from Collingbourne Ducis to Shrewsbury. The breakdown of a local culture and tradition, brought about by such extraordinary travelling, is the next subject to consider.

7
LOB

TO WRITE THIS book, and to understand the Vale of Pewsey, I have at my disposal the resources of an archives office, which is full of historical documents from the region's past; of various libraries, which store and arrange the collected wisdom of historians, archaeologists and others who have taken the same path before me; and the cornucopia of information that the internet has become. I also have the freedom to travel around the Vale, observing its buildings and landscapes in the light of what I have read. I am therefore in a more privileged position than most of the people from the periods I am writing about. If they (like me – and you too, since you have read this far) felt that it was important to interpret their surroundings, their recourse had to be to the knowledge and experience of other, usually more senior, members of their community. And by so doing they helped to nurture that body of common, unattributable information which goes by the name of folklore. A Wiltshire folklorist, Katharine Jordan, has described it thus: 'As a native of Oare, I have always known that if you run seven times round the Giant's Grave, the giant will come out. I have no idea who told me this, and family and friends from Oare all say the same: "You don't know who told you, you just know it. It's handed down."'

Sometimes such knowledge accords with 'respectable' history, sometimes it is at odds. When on a summer day in 1985 I did run around a long barrow seven times, which was a fair distance, the Devil or the giant or Old Adam (for it was Adam's Grave) did not come out (at least I did not see any of them). But then I never believed that they would. The fact is that in the past people have believed what their folklore has told them, and those beliefs have influenced their actions – and that is what matters.

Nor is folklore only to be found in the past. The appearance of circles and strange geometric patterns in ripening corn provides an

The Giant's Grave, overlooking Oare

interesting present-day parallel. Observed in Hampshire in 1976 and 1978 such phenomena proliferated during the 1980s, especially near Westbury and Avebury; and up to 1998 it was estimated that around two thousand crop circles had occurred in various places. Spectacular examples formed on 12th July 1990 in arable fields below Adam's Grave and Milk Hill, near Alton and Huish, and this part of the Vale has gone on to become celebrated by devotees of the paranormal. When in 1991 the two perpetrators of all the earlier and many of the later instances of the phenomenon revealed themselves, and demonstrated how it was done, crop circles morphed (for most people) from supernatural to artform, but tenaciously the aura of mystery and folklore has stuck. Monique Klinkenbergh created a crop circle exhibition for Wiltshire Museum in Devizes in 2014, and from 2017 has exhibited at Honeystreet, which she claims is known worldwide as 'crop circle central'. Although positive for the Vale in terms of revenue from tourism, for most local farmers the circles have morphed again, from artform to criminal damage.

Edward Thomas, who died at Arras in 1917, felt that his best poem (it is also his longest) was the one which he set in the Vale of Pewsey, and peppered with local names. He called it 'Lob', and we have already quoted a few lines from it in Chapter 4. It is a celebration of English folklore, woven around the poet's quest to find Lob, or Jack, that quintessential old countryman, whom everyone half remembers:

> The man may be like Button, or Walker, or
> Like Bottlesford, that you want, but far more

He sounds like one I saw when I was a child.
I could almost swear to him. The man was wild
And wandered. His home was where he was free.
Everybody has met one such man as he.
Does he keep clear old paths that no-one uses
But once a life-time when he loves or muses?
He is English as this gate, these flowers, this mire...

It was he, the poem continues, who under different names and
in various places, was responsible for the corpus of legends, beliefs,
remedies and superstitions which make up our folklore, and which we are
now going to dip into.

A remarkable folk-memory, recorded from various places,
including Marden, has been claimed to recall the Danish incursions into
Wiltshire of the 10th and 11th centuries. At Marden a battle took place,
the legend runs, between red-haired and black-haired men; the former
(the Danes) were victorious, and the dead were buried in a cave which no-
one dared to enter. The burial cave may in fact refer to Hatfield barrow,
which stood within the Marden henge monument until it collapsed after
excavation between 1807 and 1818. A second folk survival explaining an
archaeological site may also have some basis in Saxon reality. It came to
light during excavations at Casterley
Camp, when the archaeologists were
told of a local tradition that the
village once stood where the camp is,
but that its inhabitants moved down
and built Upavon in the valley.

Of course such a story may
simply be seen as a common-sense
explanation of a deserted settlement
overlooking a flourishing village.
Many legends are convenient
answers to questions. Why, for
instance, is the Hanging Stone
(a standing stone in a field near
Woodborough) so-called? Because,
old Lob explains, 'a man who had

*The Hanging Stone, Woodborough
(photo: Ruth Smalley)*

stolen a sheep placed it on the stone to rest, the rope by which he was carrying it being round his neck; the sheep slipped off the stone on the opposite side to that on which the man was standing, tightening the rope round his neck and so hanging him.' Sometimes Lob (in the guise this time of a correspondent to the *Gentleman's Magazine* in 1820) can even recall names and dates, such as the occupants of the Three Graves on Wickham Green near Urchfont. They were John, Jacob and Humphrey Giddons, and they died of the plague in 1644. But usually we have to be content with an explanation involving pagan gods (Woden's dyke, for Wansdyke) or giants (the two long barrows on either side of the Vale above Pewsey, called Giant's Grave) or the Devil. To him are attributed a trackway near Knap Hill, which all but disappears when you approach it, and a large chalk scar on Tan Hill, which he made with his spade; it is close to the highest point of the hill, which was sometimes known as the Devil's Church.

But some of the best stories survive without a need to explain anything. The lion on the monument on Etchilhampton Hill, for instance, when he hears the clock of Southbroom church strike midnight, leaves his pedestal and drinks from the pond in front of Stert Farm. At the same time, across the Vale on the side of Tan Hill, the chalk figure of a donkey or pony (now overgrown) used to hear All Cannings church and come down to drink at a dewpond above Cannings Cross. No such antics from the Vale's other three chalk figures. The Devizes horse, made on the side of Roundway Down in 1999, is too young for folklore. The Pewsey horse is also a (relative) youngster dating from 1937 (although he had a predecessor nearby); the Alton white horse on Milk Hill was made in about 1812, but his builder absconded with the fee before finishing the job, and was subsequently hanged for his dishonesty. That story, at least, is true.

But old Lob's best anecdotes are reserved for Bishop's Cannings, which is one of those places termed 'noodle villages' by folklorists. The supposed stupidity of its inhabitants (sometimes their feigned stupidity) has cradled numerous stories, including, it is often claimed, Wiltshire's best-known legend – that of the moonrakers. Other examples of Cannings logic include: an attempt to make the smaller of the church's two steeples grow taller by manuring it; an expedition by many villagers, equipped with ladders, to Devizes market place for a good view of an eclipse of the moon; the violent destruction of a pocket-watch in the belief that it was 'a dangerous ticktoad'; the precaution of sawing off the handle of a wheelbarrow, which had been bitten by a rabid dog; and this tale of a barrel, preserved in 1893 as an example of Wiltshire dialect: 'An thur wur a cooper ur zummat o' that, as cudden putt th'yead into a barr'l; an a telled he's bwoy to get inside and hould un up till he'd a vastened un. An when a done the bwoy hollered out droo the bung hawl, "How be I to get out, veyther?" – That bit tickled I, bless 'ee! moor'n aal on't!'

Folklore not only explains the past and provides entertainment, but also tackles a host of everyday problems, such as the weather, illness, morality, celebration and fear. Weather forecasts tend to be couched in mnemonic ditties and cryptic sayings: 'Frost in November enough

Alton white horse, seen from the road near Honeystreet canal bridge

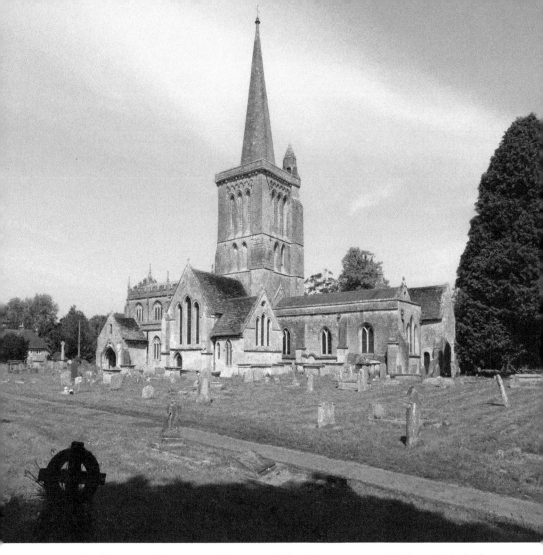

Bishop's Cannings has a magnificent parish church, a miniature Salisbury Cathedral, but the tiny second spire (over a spiral staircase) has provoked ridicule directed at 'Cannings volk'

to bear a duck, Naught else all the year excepting slush and muck', was Wootton Rivers wisdom; 'A wet May be the making o' everything', the sage of All Cannings mysteriously pronounced, and added that, 'If it rains whilst the sun is shining, the Devil is beating his grandmother – he is laughing whilst she cries'. Toothache in Pewsey was alleviated by carrying around as a charm a nine-line stanza about St Peter and Our Lord at the gate of Jerusalem, and back in All Cannings a proven remedy for warts involved rubbing them with a piece of stolen fat meat, then throwing the meat over the left shoulder at a cross-roads. Cataracts and poor eyesight could be treated by using water from a certain horse trough near Market Lavington.

Marital irregularity was another area in which folk customs participated. One device was the skimmington ride, which was generally aimed at humiliating a hen-pecked or adulterous husband. It involved parading effigies of the guilty parties outside their houses, often tied together and on horseback, to the accompaniment of an orchestra of 'rough music' comprising pots and pans and other noisy implements. At Marden in 1626 a certain Thomas Moxham, whose wife had scratched, beaten and threatened to kill him, found that (to add to his problems) he was the butt of a skimmington assembled outside his house with the approval of the lessee of Marden Farm. Other skimmingtons are recorded from Potterne and All Cannings. An almost identical procession was the Hooset Hunt, of which a local example is recorded from Burbage in 1835. Instead of mounted effigies this consisted of a horse's head, with snapping jaw and antlers affixed to it, surmounted on a draped cross. The victims, an adulterous couple, were subjected to this unsubtle form of humiliation for nine nights over a fortnight period.

The Marden affair, when presented at Quarter Sessions, was described as the *game* of skimmington, and the line between imposing folk justice and simply larking about cannot always have been clear cut. Potterne folk during the 19th century earned the sobriquet 'lambs', as an ironic reference to their unruly behaviour, or was it (as was once suggested to me) because at one time the policeman charged to keep them in order was Sergeant Wolf. And horse skulls and jawbones, like those employed in the hooset, were also used at Palm Sunday celebrations held on Martinsell until about 1860. They served as sleds for boys who raced down the breakneck hillside on them, as well as scrambling for oranges and other rough games. A similar annual gathering took place on top of Picked Hill on Good Friday. At Pewsey the village feast, of such venerable antiquity that King Alfred was popularly believed to have instigated it, was revived in 1898 as the Pewsey Carnival and Feast, and now takes pride of place every autumn in the Vale's calendar. It is a survivor of the feasts once held in most villages on the saint's day of their church dedication. A more select and better documented gathering is the annual Duck Feast, held at the Charlton Cat inn at the beginning of June. It commemorates the life and death of the poet Stephen Duck, whom we shall meet in Chapter 8, and has been held for Charlton farm labourers under the presidency of the 'Chief Duck' since 1735.

The most powerful folklore grew up around fear of the unknown, and has its roots in the barely-submerged paganism which lurked beneath village religion, at least until the onslaught of the Methodist lay preacher in the 19th century. It could presage the future, both for good – such as the Pewsey Vale practice of viewing the moon's reflection in a stream through a silk handkerchief to predict a lucky date for a wedding – and for ill. When an owl perched on a house roof in daytime it was believed that a death would shortly ensue, and the truth of this has been recorded from both Wilcot and Wootton Rivers; but the superstition is probably now forgotten, as many thatched roofs in the Easton and Milton area today are crowned by straw owls. Another harbinger was the 'antlered man' of Savernake Forest, whose appearance near Wootton Rivers in 1936 preceded the abdication of Edward VIII.

Supernatural beings like him have a considerable pedigree – indeed he sounds very similar to the Celtic horned god Cernunnos – and have become embedded in place names. Puckshipton, near Beechingstoke, which means 'the goblin's cattle-shed', is recorded as early as 1303, and Pooke Land occurs as a field name in a survey of Patney made in 1765. The 'little man in a red hat', who prowls around All Cannings, may derive from fairyland, or from Celtic mythology. The Vale, like other regions, has a number of spectral black dogs, often with eyes like saucers, dragging chains, and a tendency to vanish. Deane Water near Milton Lilbourne is a favourite haunt, but sightings have been collected from Coate, both Cannings, Urchfont, Stert and Pewsey; these too may presage death or disaster. A greyhound also figures in a supernatural story, because it repeatedly followed a courting couple from Potterne; after one muddy walk they saw it disappear towards the girl's house, where inside they discovered her mother, a reputed witch, washing mud from her legs in a shallow bath.

Stories of witches and ghosts abound in Pewsey Vale, probably not because of any special characteristic of the area, but as the result of an All Cannings woman's enthusiasm for collecting them, from friends, neighbours and Women's Institutes. Kathleen Wiltshire died shortly before her third collection of such tales was published in 1984. In her two books devoted primarily to ghosts she recorded more than 500 sightings from all over Wiltshire, but with a heavy bias towards the Vale. Consequently a rich vein of local folklore has been preserved, and only some of the more remarkable stories can be mentioned here. Monkish apparitions have been seen, for example, on the sites of two of the three religious houses in the area, Easton Priory and Upavon Priory. Likewise the site of Maggot Castle, on the wooded escarpment next to the railway line near Easterton Sands, is said to be haunted by the ghost of Seymour Wroughton, who died in 1789 as a result (according to Mrs Wiltshire) of a drink-related accident with his carriage in his own driveway. And there have been various sightings of a spectral funeral cortège processing along the Wansdyke at night, a golden crown placed on the coffin; this has been linked with the body of Guinevere being taken from Amesbury (by a somewhat round about route, it must be confessed) to Glastonbury.

Another ghost-story collector from the Vale, Sonia Smith, was told of a poltergeist at Alton Barnes attacking a lady delivering bread; a spectral old man in a brown raincoat who brought a Mini Cooper to a shuddering halt by stepping out in front of it; and a pair of beautiful disembodied hands that helped the landlady of the Nag's Head pub in Urchfont when there was too much washing-up.

Wilcot church, manor house, and the adjoining lane (see Walk 1) are the scenes of several of Mrs Wiltshire's ghost and witchcraft stories, and one which she records was first described in print as long ago as 1705. It concerns a spell cast by one Cantelow, a Devizes wizard, in about 1624 on the vicar of Wilcot. This vicar had refused access to the church belfry one night to a drunken man who wished to ring the bells. Enraged, the man consulted Cantelow, who afflicted the vicar, and anyone inside the vicarage, with the incessant sound of the bells – once outside, the ringing ceased. The end of the story, which attracted flocks of sightseers, is unknown, although the wizard was apparently imprisoned in Fisherton Gaol in Salisbury.

Some of Mrs Wiltshire's ghosts were devils. A pleasant anecdote, which would have appealed to Lob (or Jack, as he becomes known as the poem progresses), concerned the lads of Bishop's Cannings, who were illicitly playing football on Sunday near the church. 'One player gave the ball a mighty kick, and the rest of the team were amazed to see a pair of cloven hoofs appear, which kicked the ball right over the church

tower – and then disappeared! Subsequent search for the ball proved
fruitless; it was never seen again.' More sinister was the old man carrying
a pack on his back who was seen at dusk near Bishop's Cannings church.
If pursued a huge tail shot out, which almost blinded the pursuer; and
when his sight returned, the old man had gone. Such Lob-like or Jack-
like phenomena, of course, are easily explained by Cannings logic:

> When I were walking whoam to Cannings t'other night across
> the vields, there come on a bit of a vog, but 'twer not so bad that
> I couldn't zee my way, and when crossing the second vield I seed
> our Jim coming t'ords I. But on getting a bit nearer he didn't zeem
> to me to be quite like our Jim, and when we met, why, dang me,
> 'twernt neither of us.

As Edward Thomas put it:

> ...With this he disappeared
> In hazel and thorn tangled with old-man's-beard.
> But one glimpse of his back, as there he stood,
> Choosing his way, proved him of old Jack's blood,
> Young Jack perhaps, and now a Wiltshireman
> As he has often been since his days began.

8
SMALL TALK AT EASTON

ALEC AND HILDA Choules lived in a Savernake estate cottage at
Easton Royal. Alec, who was 83 when I met them in 1991, was
born in the cottage, and Hilda, a few years younger, was also a native
of Easton. They must have been almost the last of the villagers whom
Sir Henry Bashford described collectively in his description of Easton,
Wiltshire Harvest, which had been written about forty years earlier.
He lived at the White House, further up the village street, and Alec
and Hilda remembered him well. 'He was quite a decent old sort,' Alec
recalled. 'He had time to stop and talk to everybody. And you didn't have
to agree with him about everything.' Whether or not Alec knew that this
'decent old sort' had been honorary physician to the king (George VI) I
failed to discover; no-one in the village, or anywhere else, was aware until
after his death that Sir Henry had a pseudonymous *alter ego*, Augustus
Carp, whose spoof *Autobiography of a Really Good Man*, first published
in 1924, has been hailed as one of the great comic novels of the 20th
century.

Sir Henry, enjoying his retirement to stop and talk, saw the
same attitude to life in the village folk. 'All this inbred and domestically
acquired lack of anything that could be called hastiness has the
advantage of making for tolerance. Misunderstandings become less
likely.' The Wiltshireman, Sir Henry observed, 'if he falls off a bicycle or a
stack, will do it slowly and rarely hurt himself, though it may take him a
little time to make completely sure of this.'

I spent an interesting afternoon in April 1991 talking to Alec
and Hilda about the changes in village life that had occurred in their
lifetimes. Talking itself had changed. 'If only you could write how

country folk talk, you'd make a fortune,' suggested Alec. 'But you can't, there's no way on earth you can. And it's not – well, I suppose really it was a different language, the way the old folk talked when I was a kid.' In fact, five years before Alec was born a Swedish professor had published a book about the dialect of Pewsey, which he had researched by talking to old men in the Pewsey workhouse, as well as children (the 'worst speakers') at Pewsey and Oare National Schools, and a middle-aged painter and plumber who had been born in Pewsey. The professor chose the Pewsey area because he thought that here he would find a distinct idiom of Wiltshire speech.

Alec and Hilda Choules 1991

Pewsey Vale dialect was (and is) nothing to be ashamed of. Martin Pollock, brought up in Urchfont, recalled a certain Mrs Alexander, who celebrated her hundredth birthday in 1936. 'It is said that she travelled up to London as a young girl in her teens, in one of the last stage coaches to run from Bath to the metropolis, in order to learn to "speak better", but returned within a few weeks, having learnt nothing worthwhile, and concluding that the local dialect was good enough for her – or anybody, for that matter.'

Long-distance travel was unusual for a villager, of course, and Hilda reminded me how time-consuming even local journeys could be. 'We used to walk all the way to Pewsey [about 5km] to get a haircut – for sixpence. And sometimes we used to meet a lorry and get a lift home. But more often than not we had to walk both ways, just to get your hair cut. And we'd wait in the barber's there. She might be in the middle of shaving a man, and she'd say, "Just a minute, I must go and put mother [who was chair-bound] out in the garden". Well, you might see her in half an hour, or you might not. And there wasn't much you could do about it, if you had your hair half cut. You had to wait. It used to take us nearly a day.'

Among the reasons for visiting Pewsey (and it was always Pewsey: for Burbage, although closer, was viewed with suspicion by Easton folk, which apparently resulted from the violent end to a 'hurkey' match between the men of the two villages – 'I never really cottoned on to Burbage', admitted Hilda) . . . anyway, among the reasons for going to Pewsey was to visit the doctor. The strange ailments which afflicted Pewsey people were described by Mrs Haughton, the rector's daughter, in 1879. 'She's been took', was the general term for sudden illness, which might then be qualified. 'A weakly consecution', 'the lights rising' and 'the windy spasms' were fearful maladies. 'One poor woman spoke of her children as "a perfect prospect of atomies!" We were one day told by a woman that she was suffering from a new complaint now, "the giglums". But we could never discover what this complaint was, nor whether it bore any resemblance to that which immediately attacked us on hearing of it. The "gumbagurly" did duty for lumbago; St Viper's dance and St Tantrum's fire, or the Sipless, were sometimes to be met with. "Inflymation" was "most in general" – to use their own expression – supposed like all other ailments to require the assistance of wine.'

Opposite Alec and Hilda had lived an old lady (in a cottage long demolished) whose philosophy included a similar cure-all. She was in her nineties, and lived with her daughter, who was over seventy. 'They never got on, really,' Hilda told me. 'You'd see the old lady come down the steps when the daughter had gone up to the post office to get the pensions, and she'd come over here and she'd say to me. "When you go to Pewsey get me some whisky. But don't bring it back when our Beat is here, 'cos I don't want her to know." So I used to have to keep the whisky until another time the daughter went out, then she'd come across and get her whisky. She'd wrap it all up in her skirts. From here I could see right over to their place, and I could see her going up the stairs. She always hid it under her pillow.'

Drunkenness, as opposed to the occasional clandestine swig, seems not to have been a problem in Easton. For one thing, the nearest pub was the Gammon of Bacon, halfway to Milton, 'vernigh a mile away', and the smithy seems to have served instead as the village meeting place. According to the grandfather of Jack Pearce, another

Easton man who recorded his memories in print in 1996, the pub in the village, the Bleeding Horse, had been closed long ago by Lord Ailesbury, who reckoned that 'the traipse back home across the fields [from the 'Gammon'] wouldn't half cool them down'. But in many communities there was someone with a reputation for drunkenness. At Bishop's Cannings, Ida Gandy recalled, it was the roadman.

> We could watch how he worked in his worn-out way with frequent pauses for rest and refreshment. From our vantage point we were quick to note how, when one of the farmers came in sight, he would begin to labour feverishly; it was as good as a play to see how strenuously he looked all of a sudden. "Don't tire yourself, Johnny," we called once, after he had been leaning motionless on his spade for about a quarter of an hour. He turned his wide pale face and watery eyes this way and that in mute bewilderment, muttered something to himself, spat hard into the road, and fell to his work again.

At Easton the roadman was more conscientious, but he fought a losing battle, in the days before the village street had a tarmac surface, with the mess made by the cows driven twice a day along it for milking. Milking, of course, was at the heart of dairy-farming operations, and the milking machine, in Alec's opinion, was the worst thing that happened for the farm labourer.

> You see, a man milked by hand an average of about eight or ten cows in the morning and again in the afternoon. Well, if you had thirty or forty cows you needed enough labour to milk them – that would be four or five men. Now – actually there isn't a cow milked in the village – but even when there were, well one man with a milking machine milked forty or fifty cows, and so the men who had been working on the farms moved out.

Of course, village life used to revolve around the various seasons of the agricultural year. As a child in the 1890s, Ida Gandy, the rector's daughter at Bishop's Cannings, helped with the haymaking, and recalled, 'how busy and important we felt as we worked among the haymakers

Commemorative plaque to Ida Gandy, author and character of the Vale, at the Jones's Mill nature reserve, Pewsey

with the little prongs that we had cut from the lime-trees, and with what relish we drank rhubarb wine while the men quaffed their beer!' She described the practical jokes that were played, for example when the cook from the rectory sewed up the sleeves of the postman's jacket.

> The postman was a tall, thin, red-haired young man who always came to help with the haymaking, and he had left his blue coat with the brass buttons on the ground. It really was enough to make anyone burst their sides with laughter to see him trying to put it on when work was done, while cook was peeping at him from behind a tree. And then to see his eye kindle suddenly as he threw the coat down and turned and gave chase to cook! And to see cook run shrieking away from him, her face growing redder and redder at every step, until at last she fell down flop in the hay and was caught.

A more solemn description of the farming year comes from the pen of a strange and rather pathetic figure, Stephen Duck. Born at

Charlton in 1705 he worked as a farm labourer and studied literature, encouraged by a local vicar. His poem, 'The Thresher's Labour', brought him to the notice of, among others, the queen, who provided him with a house and pension, and made him a Yeoman of the Guard in 1733. His mediocre poetry was published, and brought him fame, and a good deal of scorn. He later took holy orders, but eventually drowned himself at Reading in 1756 – 'the bad rhyme to end a life that did not scan', as a modern critic noted. Duck too describes haymaking, but without the fun:

Stephen Duck

The grass again is spread upon the ground,
Till not a vacant place is to be found;
And while the parching sun-beams on it shine,
The hay-makers have time allow'd to dine.
That soon dispatch'd, they still sit on the ground;
And the brisk chat, renew'd, afresh goes round.
All talk at once; but seeming all to fear,
That what they speak, the rest will hardly hear;
Till by degrees so high their notes they strain,
A stander-by can nought distinguish plain.
So loud's their speech, and so confus'd their noise,
Scarce puzzled Echo can return the voice.
Yet, spite of this, they bravely all go on;
Each scorns to be, or seem to be, outdone.
Meanwhile the changing sky begins to lour,
And hollow winds proclaim a sudden show'r;
The tattling crowd can scarce their garments gain,
Before descends the thick impetuous rain;
Their noisy prattle all at once is done;
And to the hedge they soon for shelter run.

Although the Vale has never produced any great poets or literary figures, there have been others who have tried their hand at verse. Jack Spratt of Wootton Rivers lived from 1858 to 1932, and has been described as a village genius. His fame derived not from poetry, but from an ability to make clocks out of odds and ends. Here he describes his *magnum opus*, Wootton Rivers church clock, which, incidentally, is still working.

Wootton Rivers church clock

In 1911, at the King's Coronation,
We wanted a church clock, in commemoration:
The cost seemed too great for spare £ s d.
So I said, 'I'll make one, from odds and ends free'.
Some thought I was joking. I said, 'No, I'm not,
Let me have your scrap-heap stuff any you've got.'
They seemed to be willing, so I made a start,
And chose what I wanted each suitable part.
People gave me two large wheels nearly alike,
One did for the going side – one for the strike:
For all other wheels I made patterns of wood,
Got them cast in hard brass to make the job good.
The steel pinions I made with spindles of bikes.
A sledge hammer hits the bell when the clock strikes.
On one of three dials is 'Glory be to God'.
I used a broom handle for the pendulum rod.
It has 66lbs of lead for its bob.
My wife melted that and it was a hot job.
From April thirty to August thirty-one,
The clock was made, fixed up and everything done.

Although Alec was chapel (Hilda's family attended church) the parish church and its clergyman figured prominently in village life for everyone. Alec recalled

> The vicar and his wife were treated with a great deal of respect and they both looked and acted the part. He was tall and slow moving, but she dressed and acted the grand lady. They were about the only people in the village that we boys touched our hats to and all the girls curtsied. Once a week the vicar came to school and took a class for scripture, and wasn't above giving a boy a box in the ears. In his time he had been quite a good cricketer, and would walk to Milton on a Saturday afternoon to watch the local team. It always cramped our style when watching if he was there, and we were pleased to see him go so that we could do a bit of larking around.

Not everyone was so respectful. One of Jack Pearce's ancestors had resigned as churchwarden, telling the bishop (according to family tradition), 'Me Lord, in Easton the Parson wun't preach, the Teacher cain't teach, and the Clerk is mostly drunk, and we'm Chapel now'.

Across the fields in Milton one Victorian vicar achieved a reputation as something of a character. Parson Gale, who died in 1893, was an enthusiastic huntsman, who also served on local government bodies and as a magistrate, in addition to his clerical duties. His approach to justice was unconventional but humane, as recalled after his death in this anecdote.

> A young fellow had been summoned by the Excise Authorities for shooting game when he had only an ordinary half-guinea gun-licence. He admitted the fact, and the Bench were inclined to deal with him leniently, seeing he was a good boy as a general thing, and industrious according to his lights; but the Excise Officer had instructions to press for a conviction, and the Court [Parson Gale] accordingly addressed the culprit as follows: 'You know, Simmons, you're the victim of what I call a most unfortunate Act of Parliament, one that gives you a right to carry a gun, and then tells you you must only shoot this and that with it, and let the other alone. Now the Excise have pressed for a conviction, and we shall have to fine you a pound; but I know just how it is with you young fellows. You get your gun and go around the farm to knock over the rabbits as you have a perfect right to do, and then all of a sudden there is a whirr, and up gets a pheasant or something right in front of you; and your gun goes up to your shoulder instinctively, and you have a pull at it. I don't blame you a bit, and I should do the same thing myself.'

At Bishop's Cannings another well-loved clergyman found his relaxation in bee-keeping. His name, appropriately, was Rev C.W. Hony, and his eccentricities were affectionately recorded by his daughter, Ida Gandy.

> One Sunday, sitting in a row under the pulpit, we were spellbound to see him break off in the middle of his sermon, descend with

dignity into the nave, and without a word approach a woman who was sitting a few pews behind us. Agog with excitement, we whispered to one another, 'She must have been talking! What will he do to her?' Then, while the congregation watched with breathless attention, my father calmly removed a bee from the brim of the woman's hat, took it to the open doorway, and having set it free in the sunshine, proceeded with his sermon.

Clergymen and their wives, if they were conscientious, saw to many other needs of the community besides the purely spiritual. Augustus and Maria Hare, who settled at Alton Barnes after their marriage in 1829, began schools, gave away part of their glebe as allotments, and ran a kind of co-operative shop. They celebrated their third anniversary at Alton in June 1832 with a Sunday children's treat. Maria described the occasion to a friend:

Maria Hare

The tables and benches were spread under the cherry-tree, with chairs for the lookers-on; the jar of flowers placed upon the table; the children, consisting of twenty-four girls and seven of the little boys, arranged in order. After the second grace the children sang their hymn, and then all the little ones performed their little exercises, and so ended the feast. After the company had walked round the orchard, they took their leave, and my darling Augustus and I were left to ourselves. Whilst he betook himself to his sermon in the afternoon, I went to fulfil his duty of reading to poor Charles Gale. I do not know whether you remember him – quite a young man, with a wife and three little children, but since last summer he has never been out to work again, and is now in that slow, lingering consumption, which wastes away day by day, without any severe pain, though he suffers much from weakness.

It was a cruel irony that Maria's idyll was to be shattered during the following year when Augustus himself died of consumption.

Well-meaning attempts by the clergy and others to better the lot of the poor by improving health and hygiene were not always well received by their beneficiaries. Mrs Haughton recalls a conversation her sister Elizabeth had with an old woman in Pewsey, probably in the 1840s, whose daughter-in-law had been forced to go into the workhouse.

'And how do you think they treated my daater-la?' she inquired, trembling with indignation at the mere recollection of the insult. 'Oh, they treated her shameful! they did, 'twer downright scandalous: they put her in a bath, and washed her from head to foot.' We all rather laughed at this, and Elizabeth inquired whether the water had been cold, thinking that had possibly caused the grievance. 'Cold waater?' she cried, with horror; 'no, 'twer hot water; but such a thing had never happened to her before; it wer' a mercy she hadn't a died!'

Fifty years earlier the Pewsey overseers evidently had a rather low opinion of many of the poor to whom they paid relief. In 1797 they drew up a list of everyone they supported, over one quarter of the population. Although they did not carry it through, it seems to have been their intention at the outset to divide them into ten categories, as follows: able to work; boy; cripple; drunkard; girl; insolent and saucy; lazy; sickly; thief; and bastard. Against a few families are written complimentary remarks, such as 'all clean'; but others are condemned as 'sorry dog', 'children brought up in idleness', 'wretched', 'obstinate about the girls working', 'a bad one', 'silly', and 'to some a convenient lady' [i.e. a prostitute, presumably].

Self-help in the community has manifested itself in many ways. At Urchfont in 1929 the village set about building itself a village hall, entirely by voluntary labour. Martin Pollock recalls the efforts of his father, Hamilton Rivers Pollock, of Urchfont Manor.

Urchfont village hall

My father was a keen protagonist of the idea. Everyone was
expected to lend a hand and lay at least a few bricks, including, of
course, our family. My father's enthusiasm must have outpaced his
skill, because after an impressively extensive but markedly uneven
contribution to the south face, I remember him telling us that
he had discovered that most of his work had been secretly pulled
down and re-built later on in the evening by Mr Harding (Senior)
and helpers on the ground that it was totally unsafe!

Alec, who had been a bricklayer by trade, told a rather similar story about
the time he and a mate were detailed off to help a bishop lay a foundation
stone.

Although Mr Pollock was keen on the idea of a village hall for
Urchfont, he opposed the introduction of electricity to the village,
because of the unsightly lines and poles (the manor already had its own
private supply). At Easton Hilda remembered that the electricity came
when she was sixteen (about 1931). 'We had three lights and a plug. That
was what they put in for nothing.' 'And do you know,' Alec added, 'that
up until the electric light came, everybody had oil lamps. Nobody had a
big lamp, and of course the electric light now is on the ceiling, but the oil

The White House, Easton, former home of Sir Henry Bashford

lamp was on the table, so it was lower in the room. You could walk down through the village and hardly notice that there were lights anywhere.'

As for mains water-supply, it was a matter of some pride to Sir Henry Bashford that Easton had this amenity before its neighbour and rival, Milton. The supply provided water for most of the houses and cottages, the dairies, cattle-troughs in the fields, and a few garden taps. It had its idiosyncrasies, though.

> Most of the dairy farms are situated in the lower half of the village and, when these are requiring a considerable amount of water for the washing out of churns and the washing down of sheds, the cisterns in the upper half become empty, and this happens twice a day.' This problem, it was believed, could have been remedied by adjusting the stop-cocks. 'But unfortunately,' Sir Henry explained, 'nobody seems to know – or at any rate very exactly – where these stop-cocks are. The plans were deposited, it appears, with a former vicar, who subsequently departed, taking the plans with him, and eventually died at an address unknown.

Sir Henry himself died nearly sixty years ago, in 1961, and there is a memorial to him in Easton church. We shall let him have the last word:

> For those who die in the village, there is a small bier on four wheels. It is pulled by three men in front, the centre of whom is in charge of the steering handle, and pushed by two at the back. It is housed in a shed at the back of the churchyard, whose doors at the moment cannot be made to shut, and the mourners follow it on foot. But life-times in the village tend to be long, and it is usually the old that the bier carries, people who have grown beyond the years when ceremony matters and have died without fuss. Some day the bier itself will disintegrate, not again perhaps to be renewed. But meanwhile the little procession that, every now and then, comes down the lane doesn't seem too incongruous with its surroundings. It might almost be the roadman and a few friends with the autumn leaves.

The spring, or 'font', from which Urchfont is supposed to derive part of its name. The word is Latin in origin, and it is thought that names of this type denoted a Roman structure built around a sacred spring. Is it my imagination, or can I see in the configuration of stones a Roman maiden carrying a pitcher from which the spring flows?

PLACES TO VISIT

THERE ARE NO great national monuments, stately homes, cathedrals, ruined castles, theme parks or Tourist Attractions (with capital letters) in the Vale of Pewsey. Attractions there certainly are, in abundance, but their seductive charms are discreet, and they are not generally well known outside the local area. Anyone planning a holiday in the Vale may be assured that they will find ample scope for walking and gentle sightseeing, with fine scenery and beautiful countryside; but that they will also be within a short drive of famous landmarks, such as Avebury and Stonehenge, the attractive towns of Marlborough and Devizes (with Bath and Salisbury not too far away), and the whole of the extraordinarily diverse and much under-rated (from a tourism point of view) county of Wiltshire.

This short section confines itself to attractions within the Vale (from Potterne to Burbage, as defined earlier). Some are included in the six suggested walks which are described in the next section. Information for visitors to the Vale is available at Pewsey Heritage Centre; in Devizes at the Kennet & Avon centre on the Wharf and the Wiltshire Museum; and at Marlborough Tourist Information. Anyone can find out about everything, as you will be aware, by looking on the internet!

Natural History and Ecology

The Pewsey Downs National Nature Reserve comprises 170ha of unimproved herb-rich chalk downland along the northern escarpment of the Vale from Tan Hill to Knap Hill. There is unrestricted pedestrian access, and a small car park near Knap Hill (see Walk 4). Jones's Mill, near Pewsey, is a county nature reserve. It is a fenland habitat of 12ha formed from disused water meadows, and is managed by the Wiltshire Wildlife Trust, who have produced a leaflet about it. Access from Dursden Lane, SU170610. There are also nature reserves at Morgans Hill

(SU028673) and Roundway Covert (SU003648), bordering the western edge of our area, north of Devizes; at Scotchel, Pewsey (SU164603); and part of Savernake Forest fringes the eastern edge, at Burbage. Two very small reserves are at Peppercombe Wood on the northern edge of Urchfont, and Hat Gate, a short stretch of railway embankment north of Wootton Rivers. Countryside Stewardship arrangements provide permissive public access to a number of other interesting wildlife sites. The Kennet and Avon Canal supports a great variety of flora and fauna, including aquatic plants, fish and birds. The towpath, cuttings and embankments are also valuable wildlife habitats for insects, birds and mammals, with bankside vegetation, hedges and mature trees (see Walk 1). Wildlife management has been an important aspect of the canal restoration programme.

Rushall Farm, which extends across much of the parishes of Rushall, Charlton and Upavon, pioneered the revolution in totally organic farms in England.

Archaeological Sites

In the Vale itself there have been many important archaeological discoveries, although most (such as the major prehistoric cemetery at Potterne, and Saxon cemeteries at Pewsey and Market Lavington) have left no visible trace. However, the bank and ditch of Marden henge monument (between Marden and Beechingstoke, SU089582) may be seen from the minor road which bisects them; and the Bronze Age bowl barrow known as Swanborough Tump, which became the meeting place of its eponymous hundred, sits at the corner of a wood beside the minor road from Woodborough to Pewsey (SU130601, see Walk 1).

On the chalk hillsides prehistoric and later monuments have been less vulnerable to agriculture, and many impressive earthworks lie on or close to public rights of way. Adam's Grave (SU112634, see Chapter 1, and Walk 4), and the Giant's Grave above Milton Lilbourne (SU189582) are both chambered neolithic long barrows. Knap Hill, within the Pewsey Downs nature reserve (SU121636) is a neolithic causewayed enclosure. There are Iron Age hillforts at Rybury (SU084640), Casterley Camp (SU115535) and Martinsell (SU177640), the latter offering superb views; nearby, the other Giant's Grave, overlooking Oare (SU166632), is probably an Iron Age promontory fort defended by a dyke. What appears to be an unfinished hillfort, known as Broadbury Banks, lies on Wilsford Hill (SU092556). Finally the massive Dark Age or early Saxon linear earthwork, the Wansdyke, runs close to the top of the Vale's northern escarpment, and may be joined at several points. Public rights of way run alongside it, except in the vicinity of Shaw, and have been incorporated into the waymarked Wansdyke Path (see also Walk 4).

White Horses

Three chalk figures overlook the Vale, and another (on Tan Hill) has been lost. The Alton white horse (SU106637) lies within the Pewsey Downs nature reserve. It was made in 1812 (see Walk 4). The Pewsey white horse (SU171581) lies close to a public footpath, and in its present form dates from 1937. The Devizes white horse, recreating the lost 'Snobs Horse', but on a different site, was cut in 1999 on Roundway Down, and is well seen on the hillside when approaching from the Pewsey direction.

Villages

I cannot think of an unattractive village in the Vale of Pewsey, and so it is a little invidious to single any out for special mention. But if I were to award rosettes for some indefinable quality of picturesqueness, they would go to the following: Stert, for its setting and views (see Walk 2); Wilcot, for its estate cottages around the triangular green (see Walk 1); Wootton Rivers, for its thatch, isolation, and canalside setting; Upavon, for its miniature market place; and Urchfont, for its green and its pond. You are welcome to disagree; indeed I hope that you will test my judgement by visiting all the others as well.

Churches

This list too must be subjective, as there are so many interesting things to see. Chronologically you should begin at Alton Barnes, an atmospheric small Saxon church, which also has a gallery and pleasant woodwork, and monuments to New College men, including Augustus Hare. Whilst at Alton make your way across the fields, through village earthworks, to the redundant Alton Priors church, if only to marvel at its yew tree and to enjoy William Button's arrival outside the pearly gates. Manningford Bruce has a simple Norman church with an apsidal east end, almost no later additions, and a sympathetic Victorian restoration. The best examples of Early English architecture are on the grand scale, at Potterne and Bishop's Cannings. Both belonged to the bishops of Salisbury, and have architectural similarities to Salisbury Cathedral. Notice at Potterne also the Saxon font, and at Bishop's Cannings the painted penitential seat,

Penitential seat, Bishop's Cannings

and the little steeple alongside the main spire. Urchfont has an attractive church, with a lavishly vaulted chancel in Decorated style, of about 1320. Chirton and Marden, no more than a kilometre apart, both have churches well worth visiting. Chirton is a large church with many Norman features and an original roof of about 1200; Marden is a gem, with Norman doorway and flattened chancel arch, elegant Perpendicular tower and striking modern stained glass. The church at Easton Royal dates from a period, 1591, when churches were not normally built (see Walk 3). Finally, since this list is subjective, I include two oddities. Oare church was described by Pevsner in 1963 as the ugliest in Wiltshire, a statement he modified (sort of!) in 1975 by adding, 'in Teulon's work this kind of ugliness is an asset'. The church dates from 1857-8 and is of red and blue brick. See what you think. Stanton St Bernard church is largely of the 19th century with a medieval tower. But inside, flanking the chancel arch, is a strange ethereal painting, portraying Christ as a young Edwardian gentleman.

The Canal

Since its restoration was completed, the Kennet and Avon Canal has become the most important tourist attraction in the Vale, and many a memory of dreamy days spent cruising between the opposing horizons of Salisbury Plain and the Marlborough Downs have been, and will be, taken home and carefully preserved. Walk 1 describes a stroll along an attractive stretch of the towpath from the ornamental Ladies' Bridge to Bristow Bridge, but the whole length of the canal towpath may be walked with great enjoyment. There are picturesque wharves at Pewsey, Wootton Rivers and Honeystreet. Boats are available for private hire, public cruises and party bookings.

Walking and Outdoor Activities

The Wansdyke Path begins on Morgans Hill west of Roundway, follows Wansdyke until just north of Knap Hill, then skirts the site of Shaw before rejoining Wansdyke in West Woods and ending in Marlborough. The Tan Hill Way runs east from Knap Hill to Clench Common beyond Martinsell. A plethora of walking leaflets and booklets has been published, free and for sale, and many suggested walks are posted on the internet. I have devised six walks in the Vale, and details follow this section. Almost the entire Vale is covered by two Ordnance Survey 1:25,000 Explorer maps: no. 130, Salisbury and Stonehenge (south of an east–west line drawn through Pewsey); and no. 157, Marlborough (north of that line). A very small portion (from Milton Hill eastwards) falls on Explorer 131. Explorer maps are ideal for walkers, and for exploring in general. For cyclists one of the county's designated cycleways runs along the Vale, and is known as the Vale of Pewsey Route; it is also part of a national cycle route. It begins at Corsham and ends at Great Bedwyn, taking in Bishop's Cannings, Alton Priors, Pewsey and Wootton Rivers.

Museums

Wiltshire Museum in Devizes holds collections of international importance, and includes galleries and displays relevant to the archaeology, history and ecology of the Vale. Also in Devizes the Kennet & Avon Canal Trust has a museum in its buildings at the Wharf. Within the Vale itself the Pewsey Heritage Centre, based in a Victorian foundry, is a must, and there is also an interesting small museum at Market Lavington. Also of local interest is The Merchant's House, High Street, Marlborough (01672-511491).

WALKS

THESE SIX WALKS are intended to showcase the scenery and variety of the Vale, and so to complement the text. For the most part they use minor roads, byways and well-used footpaths and bridleways, Occasionally a major road is encountered, and then I have included a warning about traffic. Ordnance Survey Explorer 1:25,000 scale maps, sheets 130 and 157 cover almost all the area described in this book and are essential companions.

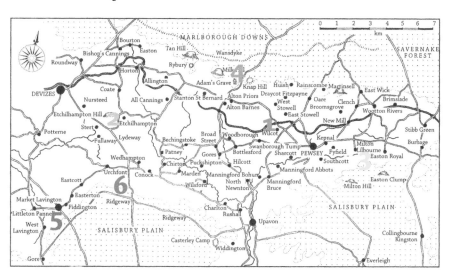

1 Wilcot

6km. Park at Wilcot Green SU 143611. A short, level walk which explores a village with an interesting settlement history, as well as an attractive stretch of the Kennet and Avon Canal. Map: O.S. Explorer 157, Marlborough.

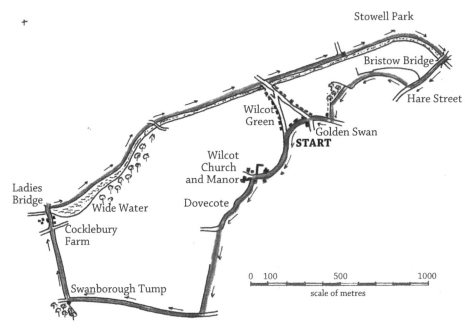

From the Golden Swan Inn (at the village cross roads) take the lane running south-west to the church.

A map of 1773 shows buildings dotted along both sides of this lane for most of its length, and more around the church than survive today. Uneven ground in the field bordering the lane on its right-hand side probably marks the site of one of the vanished houses. Because the underlying geology here is greensand this well-used lane has formed a holloway some two metres deep in places.

By the church gate the lane forks, and we bear left, so that the church and Wilcot Manor are on our right (Turn back to Chapter 7 for details of the curse imposed on the vicar of Wilcot).

This village nucleus may date from the 11th century, although the present group of buildings around the medieval church – manor house, farm, vicarage and cottages – are largely of the 18th century. But in 1086 the Domesday record for Wilcot speaks of 'a first-class house' and 'a new church'. This is quite a step up from 'the cottages by the spring', which is what Wilcot means, and which a 10th-century document suggests lay a field or two away to our left. The church and manor house are so close together, it will be noticed, as to be almost touching. In 1876 sparks from a manor house chimney are believed to have caused a fire which severely damaged the church. One post-war owner of Wilcot Manor was the actor David Niven.

Notice as you walk along the lane the circular thatched dovecote within the park which, it is estimated, may have had about 700 nest-holes for pigeons, and has a date 1737 inscribed on a lintel. Much more recently it was used as an air raid shelter.

Some 300m after bordering the churchyard the lane (no longer metalled and not a public right of way) bends right and waymarked footpaths lead off it. Walk straight on through the gateway in front of you and follow the grass division between the two unfenced fields.

The large, impressive house away to your left is Little Abbots, in Manningford parish. After about 250m a hedge and fence begin. Keep straight on to the left of them until you emerge through a metal gate on to a made-up minor road. Turn right along the road, and after 800m, where a block of woodland begins on the left, you will see the remains of Swanborough Tump, a Bronze Age barrow, and the hundred meeting place.

Take the driveway to the right opposite the barrow, which leads to Cocklebury Farm. Just beyond the pair of brick houses go through a gateway, and you will find yourself on Ladies' Bridge.

Ladies Bridge

A handsome, ornate structure, Ladies' Bridge offers a contrast to the workaday canal bridges which we shall meet later on. The lady in question was Susanna Wroughton, who owned Wilcot Manor in 1808 when the canal was being built. She is supposed to have made the building of this bridge a condition of selling her land to the canal company. Behind Ladies' Bridge, to the north-west, the distinctive profile of Picked Hill, with its triangulation point, masquerades as a miniature Glastonbury Tor. Formerly known as Cocklebury Hill it is said that crowds gathered there on Good Friday, and a fight often ensued.

Over the bridge we turn right and make our way down to the canal towpath, which we now follow for about 2.5km.

Immediately the canal broadens. This is Wide Water, another of Susanna Wroughton's requirements, and a haven for waterfowl among its rushes and the overgrown withy bed. Gradually the canal narrows, and we begin to glimpse between the trees lining the towpath the limits of the Vale as distant horizons north and south. The wooded cleft in the escarpment to our left is the meeting-place of at least seven downland tracks above Huish. The wood, Gopher Wood, is largely of oak and ash.

To our right, behind Wilcot Church amid its cluster of chimneys, we see the solid edge of Salisbury Plain above Manningford. The canal has now adopted a straight course, and after passing the brick abutments of a swing-bridge fixed to the opposite bank we arrive back at the north end of Wilcot Green.

Under Wilcot Bridge the canal continues its straight course, but now the towpath is shadowed on its left by a minor road, from which it is divided by a low, intermittent hedge. The road has been diverted, of course, by the building of the canal, but after about 400m it picks up its former course by taking a sharp left turn.

The only house here now is an ornamental thatched lodge, but this corner marks the site of a vanished hamlet, known as Stonebridge. Together with a larger settlement at East Stowell, which lay along the lane to the left, it was displaced in the early 19th century by the building of a mansion house, Stowell Lodge and its park, and by the canal. The inhabitants were rehoused in estate cottages built around Wilcot Green.

We keep to the towpath, and begin to come under the influence of Stowell Lodge.

First the lodge cottage, then an ornamental suspension bridge across the canal, which was erected in about 1845 to the design of Dredge of Bath (notice the inscription); next the park appears on our left, and the upper storeys of Stowell Lodge. As we continue our walk the house seems first to hide, but eventually reveals itself in full. It was completed in 1813 for Admiral George Montagu, the son-in-law of Susanna Wroughton. On the far edge of the park, as the canal begins to veer to the right, we can see the remains of one of a pair of pill boxes. These were part of a plan to use the canal as a line of defence in the event of a German invasion. We are now on quite an embankment, as the canal is carried across the wooded valley of a stream. This stream is described in a 10th-century charter as Ebba's Brook, and although the modern map calls it, more prosaically, Ford Brook, the old name is recalled in Avebrick Farm nearby.

Rounding the bend we encounter Bristow Bridge, where the towpath changes sides, and we leave the canal. We turn right along the minor road.

This is Hare Street, part of an ancient north-south route across the Vale, and still something of an unofficial Pewsey by-pass (hence the traffic). The canal has forced it to twist and climb away from its old fording-place across Ebba's Brook.

After 200m a waymarked footpath on our right takes us through a gate and into a meadow. Keep to the left side of this gently-curving field, below the bank created by its boundary. After about 400m a gate on the left leads into the next field, bordered by an area of woodland on the right. At its far end another gate leads out into the road, where we turn right.

On our right, in the trees, we see the end of a private lane; this was known as Nouny Lane, and is the other end of the old road to Stonebridge and East Stowell, which we saw diverted when the canal was built.

A few metres further down the modern road and we are back at Wilcot Green.

Wilcot Green is an example of a 'model' or estate village, deliberately laid out by a landowner to enhance his estate. Often the principal reason for doing this, as here, was because the existing village (East Stowell) was inconveniently close to the house and park he was building. Some of the cottages around Wilcot Green date from the late-18th century, but the ten matching pairs on the west and north-east sides are early-19th century. The school dates from 1841, and the Golden Swan Inn from about 1859.

2 Etchilhampton and Stert

9.5km. Park at the lay-by on Etchilhampton Hill SU 032599. A walk with fine views (you will regret having left your binoculars in the car!), a wide variety of scenery, and two attractive villages. It is quite long, but is set out as a figure-of-eight, so can be walked in two halves (although parking in Stert village is very restricted). It includes public footpaths across fields, which may be muddy at times. There are few waymarkers. The main road should be crossed with extreme care. Maps: O.S. Explorer 130: Salisbury and Stonehenge; and 157, Marlborough.

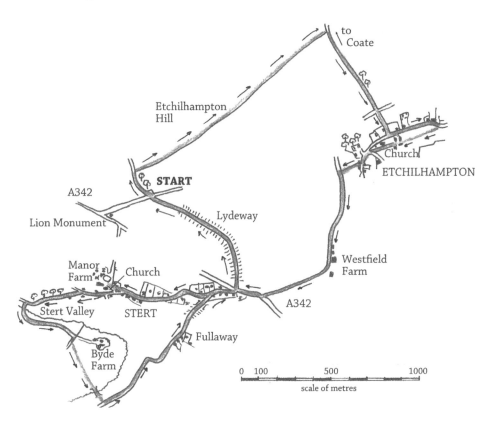

From the lay-by (300m up the lane to Etchilhampton and All Cannings, which turns off the A342 beside the lion monument) take the track up the hill. This is the old line of the Lydeway, and was the main route until 1768, when the new road (commemorated by the lion) was engineered lower down the hillside. After 150m turn right through a gate and walk up the track, looking for the triangulation point on the bank to your right at the top of Etchilhampton Hill. From here you have a true panorama, with long views in all directions.

Look eastwards first, along the Vale. Both escarpments may be seen receding into the distance. Notice the rounded profile of Martinsell beyond the Alton white horse on Milk Hill. Two smaller pointed hills, Picked Hill and Woodborough Hill, stand up from the Vale in the eastern distance, about 10km away. Like the hill you are standing on, they are chalk outliers rising from the greensand floor of the Vale. Way beyond them broods the dark Savernake Forest, and on a clear day the view extends to Ham Hill and into Berkshire above Inkpen. Now look to the south and west. Devizes and to its left the whale-like hump of Potterne Field are in the foreground; beyond it the northern edge of Salisbury Plain runs away to the rounded Bratton Camp, some 17km away, and the distant Mendip Hills mark the skyline further to the right. North of Devizes you can see the millennium white horse, cut in the hillside above the expanding industrial area alongside the Swindon Road, and to its right the Cherhill monument, an obelisk which stands above another white horse, though this cannot be seen from here. You are standing on a watershed. Rain falling on the western slope of the hill should drain into the streams which feed the Bristol Avon; on the eastern slope rain is carried to the English Channel at Christchurch by the Salisbury Avon.

Now continue along the chalk track which runs north-eastwards along the spine of Etchilhampton Hill.

You are walking along a parish and hundred boundary, and are heading straight for the low-lying area near the source of the Salisbury Avon which in late Saxon times was known as Cannings Marsh. The centres of the two territories divided by this track are All Cannings (find Alton white horse, and move your eye down and to the right – you will see All Cannings church tower in the middle distance), and Bishop's Cannings (look to your left and find the church with the spire). Each had a satellite village near the foot of the hill, Coate on the left,

Etchilhampton on the right. Tan Hill, the site of the fair, is on the horizon directly in front of you.

After a little over 1km you meet a minor road. Turn right and walk down to the T-junction, then take the footpath directly in front of you. The path emerges into the village street.

Etchilhampton is a shrunken village. East of the present settlement are the earthworks of houses deserted by the 18th century. Shrinkage continued in the 19th century, and the village broke into two halves connected only by footpaths.

Turn left into the street, passing the playing field (notice how irregular the football pitch is – houses are marked on the site on maps of 1773 and 1817), and former school (built in 1831, closed in 1970 and now the village hall). The street becomes a footpath sunk in the greensand, and then a street again. As it bends to the right by a corrugated iron shed with an elaborate weathervane (the former Baptist mission room), you will see a gate into the field on your right. Go through this, almost doubling back on yourself, into the field, and head for a stile in the opposite hedge, next to houses. Keep straight on, past the houses and along a footpath which borders the churchyard on your right.

The small church was built in the 14th century as a chapel-of-ease to All Cannings; the chancel dates from 1866. Although on entering there is a Victorian aura, the font is Norman, and there is a fine medieval sculpture of the angel Gabriel. It has been suggested that the pellets decorating the chancel arch are an all too poignant reminder to the 14th-century congregation of the terrible boil-like buboes, which were harbingers of the Black Death.

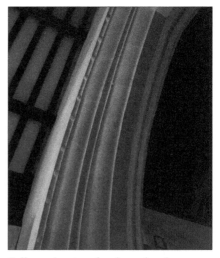

The path ends in the village street once again, next to telephone and letter boxes. Bear around to the left and left again, and look for a modern house ('Manor Orchard') on your right. Between this and the next property ('Two Trees') a narrow footpath runs up to the right and leads to a minor road. Turn left and make your way along this lane – WITH

Pellets adorning the chancel arch, Etchilhampton church

CARE, as it is well used by vehicles – until you arrive at the main road. CROSS CAREFULLY to the footpath along the other side and walk around the bend to your right until you reach the Stert turning. Walk along the lane into Stert, ignoring the left turn to Fullaway.

The lane, before it becomes a true village street, turns abruptly to its left, and crosses a former railway bridge – the deep cutting, though overgrown, is apparent on the left, but has been filled in on the right. This marks the course of the Devizes branch line, which was closed in 1966.

Pass the telephone box (currently – 2018 – in use as a very small bookshop) and Stert House, with its walled garden, on the left.

Opposite is Bitham Cottage, the first of Stert's several attractive thatched and timber-framed cottages, and like most of its neighbours a former copyhold tenement of New College, Oxford, which owned most of the village. The street descends towards a fork, and Maitlands on the left is the former Baptist chapel, closed in 1957 and greatly extended.

Take the right fork and walk past the churchyard to Manor Farm, and then double back to visit the church.

The farmhouse, which dates partly from the 17th century, was damaged by fire in 1845. Admire the pond in front of the farmhouse, and notice the hedgeline beyond, which marks the course of the vanished railway; until 1966 the Devizes branch line ran along in front of this hedge, where there is now a farm track. You can make out its course to the right also.

The church was also damaged by the 1845 fire, and rebuilt. This church, like Etchilhampton, is really only a chapel-of-ease; the mother-church is at Urchfont, 2km to the south. There is a good view from the churchyard near the church door west towards Potterne and beyond. The scenery here is different, for in fact this is where the greensand ends, and older rocks, the Gault and Kimmeridge clay, have been exposed beneath.

Leaving the church and with the churchyard on your right descend by a narrow footpath to meet a lane running past Barn Cottage. Turn sharp right and follow this lane obliquely down the hillside. Where it divides, next to railings, take the right fork (but do not turn right up a private drive). The lane now has a restricted byway sign, and passes a number of idyllic cottages on its way to a stream, with a footbridge and shallow ford. You are now in the Stert Valley, and approximately 100m lower than the top of Etchilhampton Hill.

Considering our earlier remarks about watersheds and drainage you might expect that the stream in this valley would flow westwards (left to right as you approach the ford). In fact it flows eastwards, having swept around the 'tail' of land on which Stert sits (Stert means 'tail'). The explanation is that this stream used to flow east via Fullaway into Pewsey Vale and the Salisbury Avon, but about 600m downstream from the ford, before it reached Fullaway, it has been 'captured' by another stream which was cutting back more quickly into the Gault; this has diverted it south, and then west, to Potterne Wick and beyond.

After the ford and footbridge we meet a lane and turn left along it for 400m. As this lane bends around to the right there are good views up to Stert on the left, with its church standing proud on the horizon, and away over woodland on the right towards the Lavingtons. As soon as the road straightens you are confronted by a large fence and forbidding gate. Follow the footpath sign to the right and after 50m climb a stile on your left. On the horizon you will see a prominent clump of trees. Walk straight across the field towards the clump, and as you drop down into the modest valley you will see your way across the stream, a concrete footbridge with wooden railings. By now the stream you encountered earlier has been 'captured' and is flowing away to the south-west. Ascend the hillside and turn left on to the chalk track.

The track twists and turns, and becomes a made-up lane. The houses along Stert village street perch along the ridge across the valley to your left (they must enjoy marvellous views!), and the occasional high-speed train behind the woods on your right marks the course of the railway line which was built in 1900 as a short cut to the West Country. Fullaway Farm, with slight village earthworks on either side of it, causes a deflection in the lane, and then you begin to climb off the Gault on to, or rather into, the greensand. For immediately the lane becomes a steep-sided holloway, deep enough once to carry traffic under a railway bridge, whose abutments survive.

We emerge into Stert village street again, the crossing-point of our figure-of-eight walk, and turn right to the main road junction. Cross the main road WITH THE UTMOST CARE, and you will find yourself at the start of another holloway. This is the Lydeway, here beginning its ascent of Etchilhampton Hill, and superseded in 1768 by the present main road, as commemorated by the lion monument. It is quite passable, although a little overgrown and rather muddy in places. After about 800m you will arrive back at the starting-point.

3 Milton Hill

6km. Park in Milton Lilbourne, near the village hall or church SU190604. An easy walk, using made-up roads and well-defined tracks and footpaths. Two attractive villages are explored, and a gentle climb of some 80m offers good views of the eastern half of Pewsey Vale. Parts of this walk may be muddy at certain times. Maps: O.S. Explorer 130, Salisbury and Stonehenge; 131, Romsey, Andover and Test Valley; 157, Marlborough.

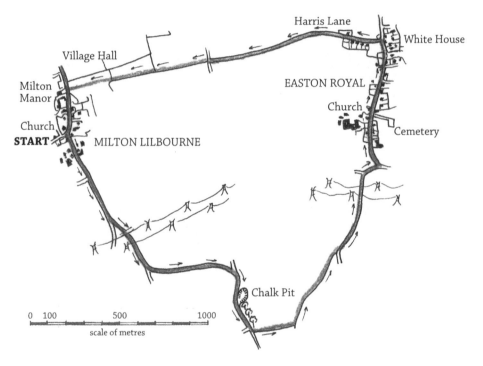

If you have parked by the village hall continue down the street, past the sarsen war memorial on your left.

You will come to Milton's nucleus, a tree-adorned grass triangle where a bridleway converges on the village street, close to the church, old vicarage, and King Hall, which may be on the site of the Lilbourne family's medieval manor house.

From this junction walk down the continuation of the village street towards the escarpment, past the (now closed) board school of 1878 on your left and farm buildings on your right. Keep to the made-up lane between trees (proclaiming unsuitablility to motor vehicles) as it begins to climb, and passes under the power lines. It bends left around a typical chalk coombe, which retains traces of lynchets on the far side, as well as the natural corrugations caused by soil creep. As the lane rounds the head of the coombe a track enters from the left.

View of Fyfield Down from Milton Hill

This is part of an old north–south route across the Vale, which here marks the parish boundary between Milton and Easton. Some three kilometres further north (behind you) it becomes the village street of Wootton Rivers.

On your left now is the entrance to a former chalk pit, and it is on the point of land above this that local people believe William Cobbett sat on his horse in 1826 to contemplate the Vale for the first time (see Chapter 2). There is no right of way to this point, but we can share the view westwards by climbing the roadside bank to a stile opposite the chalk pit entrance. We are looking right along the Vale, and can see

Picked, Woodborough and Etchilhampton Hills rising from the valley floor, the southern escarpment as far as Urchfont Clump, and the whole of the northern escarpment running away westwards. We can see beyond the Vale, too, to distant limestone hills around Bradford on Avon in west Wiltshire, over 30km away.

Continue up the lane until it levels out. A muddy track enters on the right and a line of beech trees border it on the left.

The view in front of you now is south to a wooded horizon above Everleigh. To your right the land used to be part of the common fields of Milton, which remained in strip cultivation until about 1780. Farmworkers, therefore, faced the walk you have just done every morning before their day's work.

Where the beech trees end turn left through a gap and walk alongside a shrub-obscured barbed-wire fence for some 250 metres to the far side of the field. (This short stretch along the edge of the field is permitted by the farmer although not a public right of way). From here your well-worn but overgrown bridleway runs down to the left.

As the way begins to descend it has created a deep hollow in the chalk, although to start with there is a fine view to your right. In fact, if you have brought a chocolate bar or healthy snack with you, a good place to stop for it would be on the right bank of the track just before it becomes embanked on either side. This is a sheltered spot, and it offers you the other half (northwards and eastwards) of Cobbett's view. To your right is Easton Hill, crowned by Easton Clump, which was planted in 1762 close to or on top of Bronze Age barrows and an Iron Age and Romano-British settlement site. It was here that the Easton men and the Burbage men fell out over a game of 'hurkey'. Below the clump lynchets and a diagonal trackway have been etched into the hillside, and beyond the escarpment is the straggling village of Burbage, with a dark hint of Savernake Forest on the horizon to its right and left. Easton Royal, with its squat church tower, is in front of you down the hill, and an isolated white building marks the position of the present B3087 road, the former Pewsey Herepath.

Continue down the holloway until it joins a metalled track coming in from the right, and follow this down as it flattens out under the power lines.

Now look back at the way you have come. Not only are the lynchets which you saw earlier more impressive from here, but notice that there are lynchets too on the hillside you have just descended.

The track ends in a kind of T-junction, and you must turn right through a cream gate, and then left along what becomes the village street.

Here, next to the vehicle turning bay, you cross one of the headwater streams of the Salisbury Avon, and you can imagine that this area would have become a boggy and sticky irritation in the past for long-distance travellers coming down off the chalk downland.

After the stream the village begins. Like Milton, Easton is arranged along a street which runs north for about a kilometre to the Pewsey–Burbage road. It is thought that it may in fact have been the line of the Roman road from *Cunetio* to Old Sarum. Like Milton, too, it has an attractive assortment of thatched cottages and larger village houses, and some of the most picturesque are at this southern end of the village.

Easton church is unusual in that it dates from the end of the 16th century (although the present fabric is largely Victorian). It replaced the prory church, which lay on the opposite side of the road and was demolished in 1590. Easton Priory was established in 1245, partly to serve the needs of long-distance travellers using the village street. Earthworks survive, in the field behind the present cemetery; they are probably not the remains of the friary itself, which lay closer to the road, but of garden landscaping connected with the house (demolished in the 18th century) which replaced it.

These earthworks may be seen by making a detour down a driveway and then footpath, to the right after you have passed the churchyard, and just before you reach Avon Cottage, the first house on your right. Return to the village street and walk up it as far as Harris Lane, which leads off to the left opposite the White House (Sir Henry Bashford's home until his death in 1961).

Notice on the way, among a number of attractive houses, the noble proportions of Easton House, a former farmhouse built in 1783; and the exquisite Home Farm, typical of Savernake estate ornamentation, with diamond-paned windows and a datestone of 1843.

Turn left into Harris Lane, and continue along it after it becomes a green lane with coppiced hedgebanks. The green lane runs out after about a kilometre, at the point where it meets the parish boundary lane which you encountered earlier on the hillside. But your way continues as a footpath. Cross the stile in front of you and walk along the edge of the field, admiring the view towards Martinsell and the Giant's Grave on your right, until you

come to another stile. Over the stile, across another field to a gate, and into a
third field, still heading in the same direction.

In front of you now is the imposing early-18th century brick front of
Milton Manor, with gate piers and large conical yew trees. Walk towards it
and you will emerge by a kissing gate on to the village street. There appear to
be house platforms of vanished buildings abutting the street here. Turn left
(or right if you parked by the village hall) and make your way past attractive
cottages and the precipitous churchyard bank, which has been formed by the
downcutting action of the street into the greensand.

The church is of the 13th century and later, and in the churchyard
lie Parson Gale (see Chapter 8) and some of his hunting friends.

4 Milk Hill

4.5km. Park in car park between Walkers Hill and Knap Hill, off Alton–
Kennett minor road SU116638) An easy walk offering spectacular views
across Pewsey Vale and the Marlborough Downs, and a chance to enjoy
the abundant flora of unimproved chalk grassland. Much of this walk falls
within the Pewsey Downs National Nature Reserve. Map: O.S. Explorer 157,
Marlborough.

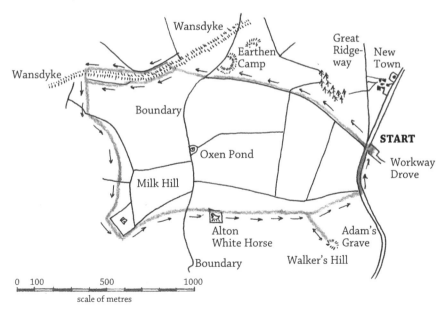

The car park adjoins the Workway Drove, which has climbed the hillside as a green track. With the Vale behind you, you can make out this drove as it continues across the minor road from Alton to Kennett (part of the 1840 turnpike road) and sweeps gently to the left up the hillside, followed by a fenceline to the right of a dry valley and to the left of a small wood.

This is your route. Cross the minor road, enter the field over a stile opposite the car park entrance, and keep to the right of the fence.

Notice the remains of lynchets and field systems on the hillside in front of you; and to your right, between the wood and the cottages alongside the minor road, you can see a straight track running away up the slope. This is the line of the Great Ridgeway, on its way to the high ground east of Avebury.

Keeping to the fenceline you will pass through a metal gate, and as the drove begins to climb notice how a slight holloway forms.

Look back from time to time. Knap Hill, a neolithic causewayed enclosure, is the spur beyond the car park, and there are parallel trackways crossing its lower slopes; to Knap Hill's right is Walker's Hill, with Adam's Grave protruding from its summit; and beyond, rising from the Vale, is Picked (i.e. 'peaked') Hill, with the edge of Salisbury Plain forming a grey line behind it.

As you approach the next gate look on your right for the upstanding earthworks of an enclosure, which is probably Iron Age in date, and contains traces of hut circles. The gate, the fence, and the slight lynchet running away to the left, mark a boundary which is mentioned in documents over a thousand years old; they even talk about this boundary going through the middle of the enclosure, which they call 'the earthen camp' or 'the old camp'. Once you are through the gate a much larger earthwork starts to become visible on the near horizon to your right. This is Wansdyke, a defensive bank and ditch probably dating from the 4th or 5th century, which runs across the Marlborough Downs and beyond. Just before you reach the gap a metal gate on your left gives access to one of the paths alongside the ditch of Wansdyke.

But before you take this path, stop to look at the view northwards across the Marlborough Downs. Silbury Hill is 4km to your north, and Avebury is behind it. To its right the high ground carries the Great Ridgeway, and further right again, almost looking along Wansdyke, you can see extensive woodland. This is West Woods above Lockeridge. Left of Silbury Hill the Cherhill Monument stands up on the horizon, with the distant Cotswolds beyond, and as you begin to walk along the path Morgans Hill, with its masts, becomes visible. Both are about 8km away.

At this point you have a choice, because there are paths on either side of Wansdyke. If you choose the more substantial one, north of the monument (beyond the gap) you will be faced with a clamber later into the ditch and out again. An easier path is that along the southern side, through the gate before the gap.

Follow one of these path alongside Wansdyke for about 500m, and as it swings gently to the left there is a good view of this massive earthwork striding up behind Tan Hill in front of you. At this point (if you have chosen the northern path) you will see on your left a gap in Wansdyke, with a stile. You must cross the ditch and head for the stile. This is where the nature reserve begins.

Enter the reserve, and follow the fenceline in front of you, keeping to its right. Climb a stile and you find yourself overlooking a great bowl-like coombe, which is often frequented by hang gliders.

To your right three hump-like hills are thrust out into the Vale; from left to right they are Clifford's Hill, Rybury (with its hillfort) and Tan Hill itself, the site of the annual fair.

After the stile turn left so as to keep to the high ground around the top of the coombe, and as you walk notice the field systems, dewpond, and parallel trackways below you. Through another stile, and then you see in front of you a fenced area of scrub and bushes. Veer to the right of this, keeping to the high ground, and head for the stile. Pewsey Vale begins to open up in front of you.

You are on Milk Hill, which vies with its neighbour Tan Hill for the honour of being the highest place in Wiltshire, 294m. As you round the spur you see villages below you in the Vale. Stanton St Bernard is the closest, and to its left the twin villages of Alton Barnes and Alton Priors, the latter's church standing prominently in the field between them. Midway between Stanton and Alton look for a boundary recorded (every twist and turn) in the Saxon charters which mentioned the old camp.

Keep walking around to the left on the hillside, and you will see the Alton white horse, cut in 1812, in front of you, and Adam's Grave on the hill beyond it. Between you and the horse is a stile, slightly down the hill, and you should head for this. It is on the Saxon boundary line we have identified. After the stile the slight path along the hillside brings you to the top of the fenced enclosure which contains the horse, and beyond it you will see the path continuing towards Adam's Grave.

View from Adam's Grave over the Altons to the Salisbury Plain escarpment

As you climb towards it the view eastwards to the dome of Martinsell opens up in front of you. You are free to walk anywhere within the nature reserve, and its limits are set out on various notice boards at its access points.

If you keep to the left of Walker's Hill and Adam's Grave you will soon see the car park down the hill in front of you. It is easiest to make for the fence and grey metal barriers which border the minor road about 200 metres south of the car park. But if you have the energy the climb up to Adam's Grave will be well rewarded.

From that vantage point you should turn to the beginning of Chapter 1 in this book, and enjoy the view with Maria Hare, the wife of the 19th-century rector of Alton Barnes. From there it is an easy scramble down the hillside and back to the car park.

The rich grassland is at its best during spring and summer, as successive wild plants come into flower, including rare orchid species and the tuberous thistle, and butterflies emerge to browse on them. But at every season this is one of the most rewarding walks in Wiltshire for anyone who likes to feel on top of the world, and who does not mind a little invigorating blusteriness.

5 The Lavingtons

8km. Park in the small car park in Market Lavington's market place, or in an unrestricted part of the High Street (SU 016542). The high-point of this walk is the long view north and east from Strawberry Hill above West Lavington, which encompasses the whole of this end of the Vale. But on the way there are hidden surprises involving water, a fine church, and the results of one family making a name for itself. Map: O.S. Explorer 130, Salisbury and Stonehenge.

From the market place walk to the right along the High Street and past the White Street/ Parsonage Lane crossroads, as far as a turning to the left, delightfully named 'The Muddle'.

Notice the urban feel of the street, a variety of shops interspersed with houses, including some of high status, and commercial premises.

Turn down The Muddle, alias New Street, and follow the footpath beside a stream until you see Broad Well, a kind of public washing or paddling place, on your left. Follow round to the right until the lane from Broad Well divides, and take the right fork which leads to a yard. In front of this yard a footpath runs to the right along the edge of a large arable field, and you should follow this, looking back occasionally for the view across to Market Lavington church. Soon you will see impressive strip lynchets etched into the hillside in front of you, and you should continue along the path, which curves to the left, becomes a track, descends among trees and then climbs again, until you are level with the lynchets.

The track becomes a holloway, and soon arrives at a cross-roads of holloways, where you should turn right, downhill, and soon you will meet a junction of two tarmac lanes. Take the right lane (Stibb Hill), and follow it down to the brick farmhouse, where it bears left, becomes Duck Street, and follows a stream opposite an attractive timbered house (The Old House). The small stream joins a larger one, which the lane crosses by a bridge and then

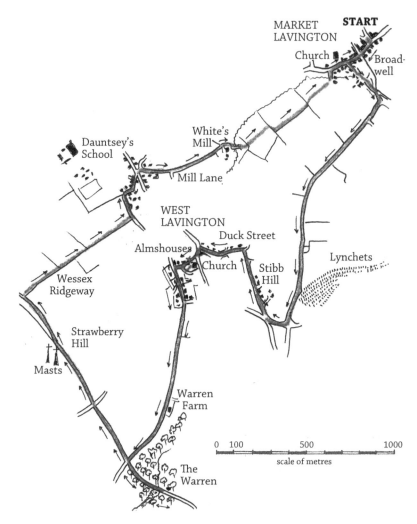

approaches the main road through West Lavington. Nearing the junction you will see a terrace of eight brick houses aslant the road junction on your left.

William Dauntsey, a successful London merchant, and major landowner in West Lavington, endowed almshouses by his will in 1542, which were erected here in 1553. They were rebuilt in brick in 1810 and extended in 1831, but had become derelict by the 1960s. They were refurbished, renamed Dauntsey Court, and are now privately owned. Notice three circular plaques, exhibiting Dauntsey's coat of arms, a woman's head, and an inscription.

At the junction TAKE EXTREME CARE, with dogs and children under close control, and cross only when you can hear no traffic (This is the main road between Devizes and Salisbury). You are heading for Church Road opposite and slightly to the left, which climbs in a cutting, and under a footbridge, to the churchyard entrance.

Dauntsey chantry chapel, West Lavington church, with letter D motif on the arch

Take time to visit the church, and notice especially the Dauntsey chantry chapel with monuments to the Danvers family (successors by marriage to the Dauntseys), decorated with a medieval 'D' motif, and the east window containing engraved glass by Simon Whistler.

On leaving the church return to the churchyard gateway at the west end, where you entered, and pass the creamy yellow manor house on your right to the thatched house at the junction. Go left into White Street, and keep straight on this, past Strawberry Hill and Rickbarton, where it turns into a track. Follow the track for 800m, past Warren Farm, until you meet a by-way at a cross-roads. Our route takes us to the right at this point, up the hill, but you may wish first to venture down the hill by the by-way to the left as far as the overgrown lake.

This area, known as the Warren, with its spectacular mature trees, was probably an adjunct to the landscaped park and grounds of the Dauntseys' West Lavington Manor, which were admired by 17th and 18th-century writers. The lakes – there are three in fact – are fed by springs which are the source of the Semington brook, an important tributary of the Bristol Avon. The Warren is a magical woodland wilderness, discreetly hidden from *hoi polloi*. Let's keep it secret!

Now retrace your steps to the cross-roads and continue climbing the hill by the by-way. As you climb you will see to the south the Salisbury Plain escarpment, sculpted by trackways and lynchets, and ahead of you two phone masts on the brow of Strawberry Hill. You should head for these, ignoring the tarmac track which joins from the right halfway along.

A few metres beyond the masts is a seat, helpfully provided by the parish council, and from here you can take in the view over Dauntsey's School and the Lavingtons beneath you, across much of Pewsey Vale, and further west beyond the Cherhill monument to west Wiltshire and the Cotswolds.

Continue on the by-way, descending now, until you reach a wooded area where motor-cycle scrambling or similar has scoured paths between the trees, and look for a footpath on your right marked Wessex Ridgeway. This takes you along the edge of a large arable field, and then around the tennis courts and sports fields of Dauntsey's School. Ignore paths to left and right until you come to a junction beside the hedges of back gardens, and then turn left. You soon come to the end of a close of modern houses (Sunnyside), which you should turn down, to bring you back to the main road.

Like the almshouses, the school owes its origins to William Dauntsey's benevolence in 1542, but not until 1895, when it was refounded as an agricultural college and removed to its present site did Dauntsey's School become significant. During the 1920s it began to expand and embarked on its career as a public school in 1930, becoming co-educational during the 1970s and now drawing its 800 students from a wide catchment area.

Cross the road (again taking great care) to the bus shelter opposite, and then enter a residential road, Sandfield. Where it forks veer right along Mill Lane, and pass an old people's home on the right and school with playing field on the left. The lane descends to White's Mill and farm buildings on the right, and you will see a small footpath ahead of you (not the path to the left). Take this and cross the stream on a footbridge, looking back to admire the timber-framed and weatherboarded mill complex.

The mill, powered by the Semington brook, probably dates from about 1700, and by 1734 it was in use both for grinding corn and for fulling cloth. It then belonged to a Devizes clothier, Richard Brooks, who wrote a manual on milling cloth and may have built for himself the fine brick house which stands nearby. The fulling machinery had gone by 1819. White's Mill is a good surviving example of a type of structure which, before the introduction of water- and then steam-driven factory-based machinery, was everywhere to be found in west Wiltshire and east Somerset, powering its all-important cloth industry.

Climb the slope by the path until it meets another. Turn left on to this and head towards a gate. You are now making your way back to Market Lavington and the church is in sight. Follow the twists and turns of the path past a rugby field on your left until you reach modern houses and a kissing gate. You can now see the High Street in front of you, turn right on to it and you will arrive back at the market place.

6 Redhorn Hill and the Font

7.5km. Park near the Pond in Urchfont village (SU041571) A walk which ascends to the highest point above Urchfont, one of the Vale's most attractive villages, and then to its lowest point, the spring or 'font' from which it acquired half its name, some 100m lower. So a walk of contrasts, of views south into the heart of the forbidding Salisbury Plain and north across the Vale, a stroll along a village street and around its pond, and a descent to an ancient, sacred place. Map: O.S. Explorer 130, Salisbury and Stonehenge.

Having enjoyed the prospect of Urchfont pond reflecting its church beyond, turn and walk away towards the junction of the village street with the B3098 road past the village, noting on the way the former school on the left and the former pub (Nags Head) on the right. Near the junction is an interesting information board about locations within the village. At the junction bear right (signed Easterton and Lavington) and follow the road until it bends right. Cross here by a small layby and take the green track beside houses, signed Stone Pit Lane.

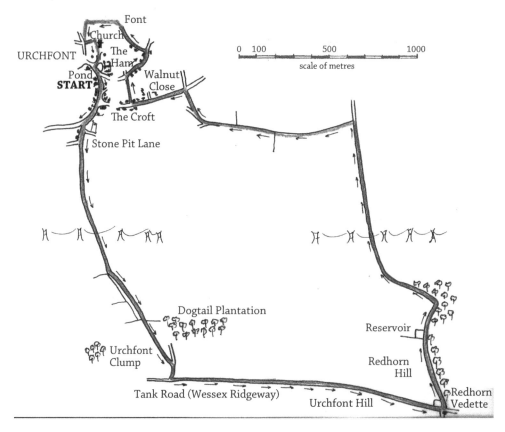

Continue along the tree-lined track in a straight line beyond the houses and within a hollow. Gradually the track climbs, and after about 600m, where it runs beneath the line of electricity pylons, you emerge into the open, with prairie-like fields on either side. Continue towards the escarpment ahead, and as you ascend look to your left at the emerging view of the Vale.

The Marlborough Downs escarpment can be seen, from Roundway in the west to Martinsell in the east, the dark eastern horizon of Savernake Forest, and the southern slopes as far as Easton Clump. The path steepens and enters a hollow edged by trees and bushes, emerging eventually near the summit, where it veers right towards a large clump of trees (Urchfont Clump or New Plantation) and joins the Wessex Ridgeway.

Turn left on to a substantial metalled roadway, one of a network across Salisbury Plain designed for tanks and military vehicles, and follow this as it climbs to the summit of Urchfont Hill, the highest point above this side of the Vale for many miles.

Notice that all the land to your right, the impact area, is out of bounds, but from the roadway and gates you can glimpse a distant south Wiltshire horizon beyond the plain; and as you ascend there are closer views of the ecologically rich wilderness that the impact area has become. There are good views too of most of the Vale, and to the west the clay Vale and towards the Cotswolds. Ahead of you is a flagpole (usually sporting a red flag) and a somewhat uncared-for hut.

This is Redhorn Vedette, which bars entry for civilians to the military Salisbury Plain ranges. It marks a significant and ancient crossroads, since here a strand of the prehistoric Great Ridgeway (parallel to which you have been walking) encounters the old main road between Devizes and Salisbury. This was in use until 1911-12, when access was restricted and then forbidden, because it crosses the military ranges used for live firing. Were you permitted to strike south along it, after walking for about 14km you would arrive at the Stonehenge visitor centre.

Stand and look at the road beyond the locked gate. Although not part of the Vale this land is part of our story, since most of the communities ranged along the southern edge of the valley had territories extending up on to this downland, which was a vital part of their farming economy. Some 4km south along this old road, and the landmark to which it aimed, is Ell Barrow, where many of the Vale parishes met and terminated. There is an information board near the vedette post describing nature conservation in the impact area.

Since our way is barred we turn and head back along the metalled road which takes us down Redhorn Hill.

Notice a covered reservoir on the left, with a view across to Roundway from an opening beyond, and then, as the road hairpins down the slope, a quarry from which the Melbourn Rock was won. This stratum of harder material separates the Lower Chalk of the hillslope from the Middle Chalk of Salisbury Plain.

The road levels and passes beneath the line of electricity pylons, and then, after some 500m the prairie fields on either side end, and just before another line of (less significant) power lines, byways are signed left and

right. Look for the way to the left (not obvious from the road but well established once identified) and follow this towards a tree-clump beyond. The sandy field here is littered with small flints which, for those with a sharp and knowing eye, must include prehistoric tools waiting to be discovered. Near the field's end the byway veers right towards a distant metal gate.

Approaching this gate it becomes apparent that it lies across the B-road, but when the road is reached do not cross. Turn left along the pavement, past the dry coombe and a turning (Walnut Close) opposite, beyond the bus shelter and almost to a left turn (The Croft). On your right are white railings, and

About 90 years old, the electricity pylons stride obtrusively along the Vale, hated by many, loved by a few

where these end are two driveways with a narrow footpath between them. Take this path and follow it until it emerges opposite a private road, The Ham. Turn right, and around a bend the lane descends, with chalk cliffs behind parking spaces on the left. Cottages stood here, abutting and tunnelling into the chalk, and this is still evident in places. Continue until a grass triangle marks a left turn (signed as a no through road with no turning area) and take this turning. Soon the tarmacked road runs out into a driveway but the track continues, and descends into Urchfont's hidden numinous secret.

This is known locally as the font, a spring which issues from the Chalk Marl to feed the Bristol Avon as one of its headwaters. As you approach you will find the spring on your right, just before a seat, and then you will see a large pond or small lake, and must explore the trees and paths and streamlets which have created this magical place.

Place-names incorporating the late-Latin word for a spring, *fontana* (there are three in Wiltshire – Teffont and Fovant, as well as Urchfont) are thought to denote the presence here in Roman times of a sacred spring, which survived into the Saxon period with some kind of masonry structure associated with it. In which case, Urchfont's 'font' has a special and very ancient history.

A path keeps to the left of the principal stream and you should follow this until the stream splashes its way into an arched culvert and you encounter another path. Turn left, keeping the treatment works to your right, and ascend by the narrow path steeply out of the cleeve, until you see the village hall on your left and emerge into a lane. Turn left past the village hall entrance, and shortly you will see steps which lead you to a path between a venerable brick wall and the churchyard railings. You will emerge beside the pond where the walk began.

The walk ends here, but it would be remiss not to visit Urchfont church, with its splendid chancel roof. Urchfont village, too, is one of the Vale's showpieces, with examples of timber-framing and fine stone and brick buildings. A stroll along its village street, to the right as you pass the pond on the left, will be well rewarded, and includes The Lamb, a pub celebrated by generations of Urchfont Manor adult students. The pub remains, although the adult college closed and was sold as a private house in 2013.

Norman doorway, Marden church

FURTHER READING

THIS BOOK HAS drawn on a wide variety of sources, primary and secondary, albeit sometimes at a rather superficial level. A lengthy apparatus of footnotes and references would be inappropriate in what is intended as a short, popular introduction to the landscape and society of a small area. I must, therefore, apologise to any reader whom I infuriate by not giving sufficient clues in the text to the sources of all my statements; you will probably find the answer in my two other books listed below. The following list is merely a selection of interesting and useful books about aspects of the Vale of Pewsey, which I offer in the hope that my work may stimulate some people to delve a little deeper.

H.W. Timperley, *The Vale of Pewsey*, 1954, is a pleasant mixture of astute observation, leisurely botanising and gentle local history. It is the only previous book to have been devoted specifically to the Vale, but does not cover the Lavington area.

Scholarly histories of all parishes in the Vale are provided by volumes of the *Victoria History of Wiltshire*. Volume 7 (1953) includes Bishop's Cannings, Potterne and West Lavington; volume 11 (1980) has Alton Priors and Patney; volume 10 (1975) deals with everywhere else, except Pewsey, Easton, Milton, Wootton and Burbage, which are in volume 16 (1999). The general volumes (1-5) also have much to say about the Vale, including archaeology, agriculture, roads and railways, population and religious houses.

I have written two books which contain brief histories of all the parishes in the former Kennet District Council area: *Marlborough and Eastern Wiltshire* (2001) includes Burbage. Every other parish in the Vale is described in *Devizes and Central Wiltshire* (2003).

Reminiscences, diaries and the like can be very informative, as well as entertaining. H.H. Bashford, *Wiltshire Harvest*, 1953; and Jack Pearce, *Accounts and Recollections*, 1996 (both Easton Royal); Ida Gandy, *A Wiltshire Childhood*, 1929, reprinted 1988 (Bishop's Cannings); 'Peter

Gurney' [C.S. Smith], *Shepherd Lore*, 1985; A.J.C. Hare, *Memorials of a Quiet Life*, 1872 (Alton Barnes); Mrs Haughton, *In a Wiltshire Valley*, 1879, reprinted 1980 (Pewsey); and T. Smith, *Potterne 1850-1900*, 1983, are all well worth reading. A number of parishes produced millennium histories or descriptions of their communities.

Useful works on specific subjects include the following: **Agriculture**: A.H. Fry, *Land Utilisation Survey: Wiltshire*, 1940; B. Wookey, *Rushall: the Story of an Organic Farm*, 1987; **Archaeology and Early History:** P. Ellis (ed.), *Roman Wiltshire and After*, 2001; G. Brown *et al* (eds.), *The Avebury Landscape*, 2005; P Williams and R. Newman, *Market Lavington, Wiltshire: an Anglo-Saxon Cemetery and Settlement*, 2006; F.K. Annable and B.N. Eagles, *The Anglo-Saxon Cemetery at Blacknall Field, Pewsey, Wiltshire*, 2010; S. Draper, *Landscape, Settlement and Society in Roman and Early Medieval Wiltshire*, 2006; **Architecture**: N. Pevsner and B. Cherry, *Wiltshire,* 2nd ed., 1975 (note that a fully revised and expanded edition of this volume in the Buildings of England series is due to be published in 2019, edited by J. Orbach); P.M. Slocombe, *Wiltshire Farmhouses and Cottages, 1500-1850*, 1988; J. Chandler and D. Parker, *The Church in Wiltshire*, 2006; **Canal**: K.R. Clew, *The Kennet and Avon Canal*, 3rd ed., 1985; **Folklore**: K.M. Jordan, *The Folklore of Ancient Wiltshire*, 1990; K.M. Jordan, *The Haunted* Landscape, 2000; K. Wiltshire, *Ghosts and Legends of the Wiltshire Countryside*, 1973; K. Wiltshire, *The Folklore of Wiltshire*, 1975; K. Wiltshire, *More Ghosts and Legends of the Wiltshire Countryside*, 1984; S. Smith, *Wiltshire Stories of the Supernatural*, 2007; **Geology and Landscape**: R.S. Barron, *The Geology of Wiltshire: a Field Guide*, 1976; D.C. Findlay, *Soils in Wiltshire II: Devizes*, 1986; I. Geddes, *Hidden Depths: Wiltshire's Geology and Landscapes*, 2000; S. Hannath, *Chalk and Cheese*, 2014; **Medieval History**: J. Hare, *A Prospering Society: Wiltshire in the Later Middle Ages*, 2011; **Photographs**: D. Buxton, *Around Devizes in Old Photographs*, 1990; R. Pope, *The Pewsey Vale in Old Photographs*, 1988; **Social Life**: H.E. Bracey, *Social Provision in Rural Wiltshire*, 1952.

In addition, anyone embarking on a local history study in Wiltshire should be aware of the following serial publications: *Wiltshire Archaeological and Natural History Magazine; Wiltshire Folklife; Wiltshire Notes and Queries; Wiltshire Record Society.*

INDEX

This is an index of place names, personal names and selected subjects. Most places outside the Vale have been omitted.

Stanton St Bernard, chancel arch painting